THE CREATIVE TRAINER

Latest titles in the McGraw-Hill Training Series

EVALUATING TRAINING EFFECTIVENESS 2nd edition
Benchmarking your Training Activity Against Best Practice
Peter Bramley   ISBN 0-07-709028-4
DEVELOPING A LEARNING CULTURE
Empowering People to Deliver Quality, Innovation and Long-term Success
Sue Jones   ISBN 0-07-707983-3
THE CREATIVE TRAINER
Holistic Facilitation Skills for Accelerated Learning
Michael Lawlor and Peter Handley   ISBN 0-07-709030-6
DEVELOPING EFFECTIVE TRAINING SKILLS 2nd edition
A Practical Guide to Designing and Delivering Group Training
Tony Pont   ISBN 0-07-709143-4
CROSS-CULTURAL TEAM BUILDING
Guidelines for More Effective Communication and Negotiation
Mel Berger   ISBN 0-07-707919-1
LEARNING TO CHANGE
A Resource for Trainers, Managers and Learners Based on Self-Organized Learning
Sheila Harri-Augstein and Ian M. Webb   ISBN 0-07-707896-9
ASSESSMENT AND DEVELOPMENT IN EUROPE
Adding Value to Individuals and Organizations
Edited by Mac Bolton   ISBN 0-07-707928-0
PRACTICAL INSTRUCTIONAL DESIGN FOR OPEN LEARNING
MATERIALS
A Modular Course Covering Open Learning, Computer-based Training and
Multimedia
Nigel Harrison   ISBN 0-07-709055-1
DELIVERING IN-HOUSE OUTPLACEMENT
A Practical Guide for Trainers, Managers and Personnel Specialists
Alan Jones   ISBN 0-07-707895-0
FACILITATION
Providing Opportunities For Learning
Trevor Bentley   ISBN 0-07-707684-2
DEVELOPMENT CENTRES
Realizing the Potential of Your Employees Through Assessment and Development
Geoff Lee and David Beard   ISBN 0-07-707785-7
DEVELOPING DIRECTORS
Building an Effective Boardroom Team
Colin Coulson-Thomas   ISBN 0-07-707590-0
MANAGING THE TRAINING PROCESS
Putting the Basics into Practice
Mike Wills   ISBN 0-07-707806-3
RESOURCE-BASED LEARNING
Using Open and Flexible Resources for Continuous Development
Julie Dorrell   ISBN 0-07-707692-3

Details of these and other titles in the series are available from:

The Product Manager, Professional Books, McGraw-Hill Book Company Europe,
Shoppenhangers Road, Maidenhead, Berkshire SL6 2QL, United Kingdom
Tel: 01628 23432 Fax: 01628 770224

The Creative Trainer

Holistic facilitation skills for accelerated learning

Michael Lawlor and Peter Handley

The McGraw-Hill Companies

London · New York · St Louis · San Francisco · Auckland
Bogotá · Caracas · Lisbon · Madrid · Mexico · Milan
Montreal · New Delhi · Panama · Paris · San Juan · São Paulo
Singapore · Sydney · Tokyo · Toronto

Published by
McGraw-Hill Publishing Company
Shoppenhangers Road, Maidenhead, Berkshire SL6 2QL, England
Telephone: 01628 23432
Fax: 01628 770224

British Library Cataloguing in Publication Data
The creative trainer: holistic facilitation skills for
    accelerated learning.—(McGraw-Hill training series)
    1. Employees—Training of
    I. Handley, Peter
    658.3'124

ISBN 0-07-709030-6

Library of Congress Cataloging-in-publication Data
Lawlor, Michel.
    The creative trainer: holistic facilitation skills for
accelerated learning / Michel Lawlor and Peter Handley.
        p.   cm.— (The McGraw-Hill training series)
    Includes bibliographical references and index.
    ISBN 0-07-709030-6 (pbk.)
    1. Employees– Training of.   2. Organizational learning.
    I. Handley, Peter. II. Title. III. Series.
    HF5549.5.T7L34   1996
    658.3'12404–dc20   95-49800
                                                  CIP

McGraw-Hill

A Division of The McGraw·Hill Companies

 34 CUP 98

Typeset by BookEns Limited, Royston, Herts.
and printed and bound in Great Britain at the University Press, Cambridge

Printed on permanent paper in compliance with ISO Standard 9706.

To Peter O'Connell, the first Chairman of SEAL (The Society for Effective Affective Learning), and to all those who gave their time and energy to foster the growth of the society and the ideals it stands for.

Contents

Series preface   xi
About the series editor   xiii
Acknowledgements   xiv
About the authors   xv
Preface   xvii
Introduction: 'The Glospot story'   xxiii

Part 1   Fundamentals   1

1   A new approach to training   3
     Brain capacity   4
     Barriers   4
     Right and left brain   5
     The limbic system   5
     Sensory modalities   6
     Visualization   6
     The body-mind link   7
     Multiple intelligences   7
     Notes and references   8

2   Creative facilitation   10
     The audience   12
     Atmosphere   12
     The body and energy levels   12
     Visualization   12
     Inner awareness   13
     Learner-centred orientation   13
     Rapport   13
     Technology   14
     Notes and references   15

Part 2   Building a training course   17

3   The four-quadrant teaching cycle—An overview   19
     Quadrant 1 Preparation   21
     Quadrant 2 Presentation   22

Quadrant 3 Practice   23
Quadrant 4 Performance   23
Notes and references   24

4 Quadrant 1—Preparation   **26**
Preparing the learner for the learning event   27
Creating a positive learning environment   28
Connecting and engaging   30
Conclusion   32
Notes and references   32

5 Quadrant 2—Presentation   **35**
Acting out a dialogue   37
Giving a concert reading   39
Telling a story   40
Making a challenging statement   40
Playing an audio or video tape   40
Involving the group with lists   41
Using visualization   41

6 Quadrant 3—Practice   **45**
Group dynamic   46
Individual activities   48
Partnered activities   49
Team-based activities   50
Notes and references   53

7 Quadrant 4—Performance   **55**
Individual activities   58
Partnered activities   58
Team-based activities   59
Notes and references   60

Part 3   The building blocks   **63**

8 Thinking and learning styles   **65**
Herrmann Brain Dominance Instrument (HBDI)   67
Multiple intelligences   70
Notes and references   72

**9 The body–mind link and the management of stress—
   Physical and mental harmony**   **76**
Correct seating position   78
Breathing   78
Relaxation   79
Emotional calmness   81
Concentration   81

Energy 82
Life style 83
Notes and references 84

10 Suggestion **86**
Double-planeness 87
Authority 88
Environment 89
Concert state 89
The inner child 90
Language 91
Visualization and affirmation 91
Notes and references 92

11 Voice production and body movement **94**
Use of the body 96
The Alexander Technique 97
Voice production 99
Notes and references 101

12 Inner awareness **103**
Physical and emotional state 104
Brain function 105
Notes 107

13 Visualization **109**
Preparing for visualization 111
Applications of visualization 113
Notes and references 117

Part 4 The learner's perspective 119

14 Study skills 1 **121**
Determining individual learning styles 122
Before the study session 122
Notes and references 125

15 Study skills 2 **127**
During the study session 128
After the study session 133
Notes and references 134

Part 5 Transforming the organization 137

16 Creating **139**
Generating structural tension 141
Notes and references 144

17   Towards a learning organization   **146**
   Personal mastery (The first discipline)   147
   Mental models (The second discipline)   148
   Shared vision (The third discipline)   148
   Team learning (The fourth discipline)   148
   Systems thinking (The fifth discipline)   150
   Notes and references   151

Part 6   The method in action   **153**

18   Case studies   **155**
   Case study 18.1 Allied Dunbar   155
   Preparation   156
   Presentation   157
   Practice   158
   Performance   159
   Case study 18.2 Robson Rhodes   160
   Preparation   161
   Presentation   162
   Practice   165
   Performance   165
   Notes and references   166

Appendix A   Music   **167**
Appendix B   How clear is your mind's eye?   **169**
Appendix C   Awareness chart   **171**
Appendix D   Useful addresses   **172**

Bibliography   **174**

Index   **177**

Series preface

Training and development are now firmly centre stage in most organizations, if not all. Nothing unusual in that—for some organizations. They have always seen training and development as part of the heart of their businesses—but more and more must see it that same way.

The demographic trends through the 1990s will inject into the marketplace severe competition for good people who will need good training. Young people without conventional qualifications, skilled workers in redundant crafts, people out of work, women wishing to return to work—all will require excellent training to fit them to meet the job demands of the 1990s and beyond.

But excellent training does not spring from what we have done well in the past. T&D specialists are in a new ball game. 'Maintenance' training—training to keep up skill levels to do what we have always done—will be less in demand. Rather, organization, work and market change training are now much more important and will remain so for some time. Changing organizations and people is no easy task, requiring special skills and expertise which, sadly, many T&D specialists do not possess.

To work as a 'change' specialist requires us to get to centre stage—to the heart of the company's business. This means we have to ask about future goals and strategies, and even be involved in their development, at least as far as T&D policies are concerned.

This demands excellent communication skills, political expertise, negotiating ability, diagnostic skills—indeed, all the skills a good internal consultant requires.

The implications for T&D specialists are considerable. It is not enough merely to be skilled in the basics of training, we must also begin to act like business people and to think in business terms and talk the language of business. We must be able to resource training not just from within but by using the vast array of external resources. We must be able to manage our activities as well as any other manager. We must share in the creation and communication of the company's vision. We must never let the goals of the company out of our sight.

In short, we may have to grow and change with the business. It will be hard. We shall have to demonstrate not only relevance but also value for money and achievement of results. We shall be our own boss, as accountable for results as any other line manager, and we shall have to deal with fewer internal resources.

The challenge is on, as many T&D specialists have demonstrated to me over the past few years. We need to be capable of meeting that challenge. This is why McGraw-Hill Book Company Europe have planned and launched this major new training series—to help us meet that challenge.

The series covers all aspects of T&D and provides the knowledge base from which we can develop plans to meet the challenge. They are practical books for the professional person. They are a starting point for planning our journey into the twenty-first century.

Use them well. Don't just read them. Highlight key ideas, thoughts, action pointers or whatever, and have a go at doing something with them. Through experimentation we evolve; through stagnation we die.

I know that all the authors in the McGraw-Hill Training Series would want me to wish you good luck. Have a great journey into the twenty-first century.

ROGER BENNETT
Series Editor

About the series editor

Roger Bennett has over 20 years' experience in training, management education, research and consulting. He has long been involved with trainer training and trainer effectiveness. He has carried out research into trainer effectiveness, and conducted workshops, seminars, and conferences on the subject around the world. He has written extensively on the subject including the book *Improving Trainer Effectiveness*, Gower. His work has taken him all over the world and has involved directors of companies as well as managers and trainers.

Dr Bennett has worked in engineering, several business schools (including the International Management Centre, where he launched the UK's first masters degree in T&D), and has been a board director of two companies. He is the editor of the *Journal of European Industrial Training* and was series editor of the ITD's *Get In There* workbook and video package for the managers of training departments. He now runs his own business called The Management Development Consultancy.

Acknowledgements

The authors would like to thank the following for their assistance:

David Meier, for his inspiration and encouragement and for providing the model of the four quadrant cycle.

Vic Wiltshire, who drew the cartoons.

Emily Lawlor, who drew the mind maps.

Vanda North, for her help in developing the mind maps.

Jill Johnson and Robin How for reading the manuscript and for making many helpful suggestions.

Mike Finch of Winchcombe Pottery, Winchcombe, Glos., for providing background material for the Glospot story.

About the authors

Michael Lawlor has extensive training and export management experience in both UK and international companies. He ran his own company, a language school for businessmen, for 26 years, prior to becoming a full-time management trainer. He is Director of the Centre for Inner Development in Business Ltd. and President of SEAL (The Society for Effective Affective Learning). He is a Fellow of the Royal Society of Arts, of the Institute of Linguists and of the Institute of Personnel and Development. He is the author of five books: *Inner Track Learning, Negotiating with Insight, Export Marketing in French, Export Marketing in German* and *Unfinished Business in Bangkok* (an E.F.L. course book/reader).

Peter Handley has broad experience of working in manufacturing, sales and service organizations. Trained as an engineer, his last two posts were as Training and Development Manager with G.E.C. and then with Hewlett Packard. With the latter he was also Quality Training Manager with responsibilities for the development of innovative quality training programmes. He is now self-employed with Kingwood Centre for Learning, providing leading professional training qualifications, management skills workshops and personal development programmes. He is a Member of the Institute of Personnel and Development and a Fellow of the Institute of Information Technology Training and holds a Masters Degree in Management Learning from the University of Lancaster.

Preface

This book is about facilitating learning. It is for trainers who want to become facilitators in the widest and best sense of the word. But it is not just about 'making easy', which is the dictionary definition of facilitating. It is about the empowering and transformation of individuals, of giving them an opportunity to find their uniqueness and their creativity. By doing this individuals begin to realize their potential. They become the agents of change in their organizations.

The needs of organizations in the industrial age were for manpower to operate production lines. The task of trainers was to turn out workers and office staff with the minimum level of skill required. Work was mindless and soulless. People were treated as units of production. The structure was hierarchical, with little contact between white- and blue-collar workers.

In this situation training was either curriculum centred or trainer centred. Curriculum centred training was focused on delivering the knowledge and skills required to do a particular job, which was unlikely to change during the lifetime of the employee. Trainer centred training was similar, but with the emphasis on the knowledge and expertise of the trainer. In neither case was there any attempt to cater for the differences in learning styles or personal goals of individuals or to develop their potential.

Today the needs of organizations are different, although in many respects training methods have not changed. In an age when information technology and sophisticated manufacturing processes are becoming predominant, the need is for people who can think for themselves, who can adapt and learn new skills quickly and who have personal development goals which are aligned with those of their organization.

To cope with these needs, training should move from curriculum or trainer centred to learner centred. The training methods described in this book are essentially learner centred, although they rely on a high degree of expertise and commitment on the part of the trainer. Learner centred training takes into account three factors:

1 The goals and motivations of the learners.
2 The learning styles, the past learning experience and possible learning blocks of the learners.
3 The environment in which learning takes place.

All of these are addressed in the method described in this book. The method is based mainly on Accelerated Learning and on the work of Georgi Lozanov, but the authors have also been influenced by John Heron and Carl Rogers. Their innovative ideas on learning provide the conceptual framework. A number of other methods are included, in order to widen the range of possibilities for creativity and effectiveness in training. These include Neuro-Linguistic Programming (Bandler and Grinder), Accelerated Learning Systems 2000 (Colin Rose), Inner Track Learning (Michael Lawlor), Technologies for Creating (Robert Fritz), Educational Kinesiology or Brain Gym (Paul and Gail Dennison), the Inner Game (Timothy Gallwey), the Alexander Technique (Mathias Alexander), Autogenic Training (J.W. Schultz), Office Yoga (Julie Friedberger), Mind Mapping (Tony Buzan) and the work of David Meier of the Center for Accelerated Learning in Wisconsin.

The book puts at the disposal of training officers and managers the results of the brain research which in recent years has transformed ideas about learning. It is also a practical guide to using this knowledge in the classroom. Briefly, the discoveries about the brain which are relevant to training and which are dealt with in this book, are:

1 **The brain has much greater potential than is generally believed**. Researchers now think that few people use more than one per cent of their brain's capacity for memory and creative thinking. This capacity can be used more fully by the deliberate activation of parts of the brain not habitually used.
2 **The unused capacity of the brain is difficult to access because of limiting beliefs**. These can be overcome by a variety of indirect suggestive elements, such as the classroom environment, a supportive group, the authority of the trainer and guided visualization (see Chapter 10).
3 **The cerebral cortex of the brain is split into two halves**. The left half tends to think analytically, logically and linearly. The right half is concerned more with imagination, creativity and intuition. Most people have a tendency to think more with one half than the other. To be effective, lessons need to be delivered in a way which enables both types of thinker to learn (see Chapter 8).
4 **In the mid-brain there is an area known as the limbic system which is the seat of the emotions**. It is only if incoming information has some emotional content that the limbic system will allow it to be passed to the long-term memory (see Chapter 8).
5 **The outside world is perceived by the brain through the senses**—chiefly visual, auditory or kinesthetic (physical)—and most people have a preference as to which one of these senses they use.

To learn effectively they need to have information presented to them in a way which allows their preferred sense or senses to become involved (see Chapter 8).

6 **Visualization or mental imaging can improve performance and motivation.** If people can learn to create clear, multi-sensory images of the action they wish to perform or the goal they wish to achieve, they call on the reserve power of their subconscious mind and often achieve results far beyond their original capability. This concept has been shown dramatically in the improvement of performance in sport through the 'Inner Game' (see Chapter 13).

7 **There is a strong link between the body and the functioning of the brain.** Mental processes take place more effectively if the body is relaxed, the posture is upright and balanced and the emotions are calm (see Chapter 9).

8 **Intelligence can be defined in ways other than by the traditional mathematical/logical and linguistic criteria.** There are in addition at least five other types of intelligence—visual/spatial, musical, kinesthetic, inter-personal and intra-personal. All of them can be made use of in training (see Chapters 8 and 15).

A useful framework into which these concepts can be placed is that provided by John Heron, formerly head of the Human Potential Resources Group at the University of Surrey and author of *The Facilitators' Handbook*. Of particular relevance is his three-stage model of facilitation. This provides for the gradual transference of leadership from hierarchical, through co-operative to autonomous group functioning. It also emphasizes the importance of feeling in learning, an area widely ignored in most training. The Heron model underlies the four quadrant cycle, developed by David Meier and described in Chapters 3 to 7.

Another much ignored but increasingly important area of training and management is the ethical dimension. Ethics and moral values can not be imposed on individuals. But people can be given the opportunity of getting in touch with higher values by periods of silent reflection and discussion. They can also be influenced by example and by the values underlying the culture of the organization (see Chapter 7).

At the time of writing, a large insurance company has just been fined £325 000 and has had to withdraw all its salespeople from the field because they were found to have been giving advice which was more in line with high commission than with benefits for the client. Organizations ignore ethics at their peril.

The learner centred training described in this book leads naturally towards the creation of a Learning Organization. This has been defined as 'an organization which facilitates the learning of all its members and continuously transforms itself' (Pedler, Boydell and Burgoyne).

To add interest to the book and to show how each of the subjects covered applies in the world outside the classroom, there is a story running throughout. It is the story of Glospot Ltd., a medium-sized pottery near Cheltenham in Gloucestershire. At the beginning of each chapter there is a short dialogue. This traces the progress of a training consultant called Tony Wakeman in his task of turning training in the company into a learner centred operation and eventually the company itself into a learning organization. This will enable it to come to terms with the changes it needs to make in order to survive. The story of Glospot and an outline of its organization is given below.

The organigram of the company shown in Figure I1.1 may seem somewhat hierarchical and top-heavy to the eyes of trainers working in 'lean' organizations, which have achieved a flatter structure. However, this is one of the aspects of the company which is likely to change as it moves towards becoming a learning organization.

There is a second reason for including these dialogues. They act as a model of how this method of training can be delivered in the classroom. Because they involve people, they have an emotional content. This awakens the interest of the right brain and the limbic system. Unless a trainer can do this, the information which they impart is likely to be quickly forgotten. Even if it is remembered, it is unlikely to produce enthusiasm or motivation. But a lesson which contains human interest of this kind at the beginning is on a different level. It involves the whole brain.

You may find it worth glancing at the Glospot story now, before you start the first chapter. If the idea of reading imaginary dialogues does not appeal to you, you can skip the page on which they are written at the beginning and get straight into the content of the chapter. On the other hand, if you like the story, you might like to get an overview of the book by reading all the dialogues to start with. This may tell you something about your brain dominance! (see Chapter 8).

At the end of the book are case studies from two real companies which have successfully used accelerated learning in their training. They are Allied Dunbar and Robson Rhodes.

You will notice that at the end of each chapter there is a mind map. These mind maps are included to illustrate one of the learning methods advocated in the book and to assist you in getting an overview of the contents. You may find it a useful memory aid to colour in these mind maps with a felt tipped pen or crayon.

Neuro-Linguistic Programming (NLP)

NLP is a set of guiding principles, attitudes and techniques that enable you to change—or eliminate—behaviour patterns as you wish. NLP describes the dynamics between the brain (neuro) and language (linguistic) and how the interplay 'programmes' our behaviour. It began in the early 1970s with Bandler and Grinder, who explored how to model excellence by closely observing three highly successful therapists at work. The process they used was modelling—relying not only on what the three thought they were doing, but on the pattern of language and behaviour they actually used. The two researchers then tried out these same patterns themselves and developed strategies to pass them on to others. In short, NLP is about having the awareness and skills to know what motivates and influences others.

Details of NLP courses available in the UK can be obtained from the Association of Neuro-Linguistic Programming (see Appendix D—Useful Addresses).

Matching

Matching is an NLP term meaning creating rapport with another person by mirroring in a discreet way some of the ways in which they are using their body, such as their posture, gestures and breathing. Once rapport has been established it can be followed by 'leading'. This means changing the use of your own body so that the other person unconsciously follows your lead. In this way you can help the other person achieve a body posture which may be more open and receptive.

Mind maps

Mind maps constitute a non-linear method of note taking which links key words and ideas. The method was pioneered by Tony Buzan, who has done much to introduce and popularize study skills such as memory training and speed reading.[1]

Accelerated Learning or suggestopedia

Accelerated Learning derives from suggestopedia, a method of teaching and learning which fosters positive psychological growth in addition to imparting information and assisting memory. Developed by the Bulgarian doctor and psychotherapist Georgi Lozanov, the creator of suggestopedia, it became known in the West in the early 1970s. His aim was to demonstrate the considerable untapped reserve powers of the brain, and he chose language teaching in order to achieve this. The method has since been adapted and expanded in the West and is used in many other fields. In its new form suggestopedia is known as Superlearning or Accelerated Learning.

---

[1] Acknowledgement is made by the authors to SEAL for use of the definitions of NLP, suggestopedia and mind mapping. A comprehensive Glossary of Terms can be obtained from Forge House (see Appendix D for address).

Introduction: 'The Glospot story'[1]

Glospot was founded in 1926 by John Bird. His aim was to produce handcrafted pottery which was both attractive and useful, at a price that ordinary people could afford. The tradition of handmade pottery had almost died out at that time, due to the rise of moulding technology and automation. Pots produced in this way, mainly in the Stoke-on-Trent area, were cheaper but lacked aesthetic qualities and individuality, unless they were very expensive.

John Bird had difficulty in finding anyone to teach him the skill of throwing, glazing and wood-firing pots in the old tradition, but eventually he found an old man in Somerset called Elijah Beach, who was still practising his trade. John apprenticed himself to the old man in 1919, and after seven years felt that he knew enough of the craft to start his own pottery. He found a derelict farm building in Wychford in Gloucestershire, which was available for a peppercorn rent and set himself up with a wheel and kiln, bought with a loan from an indulgent but sceptical father.

After six years of hard work and very little income, John had established himself and was able to employ two young assistants. He married in 1934 and had two children, the eldest of whom, Michael, was interested in pottery and learned the craft and the business. In 1958 Michael married Jill Goodfellow, the daughter of a local potter and herself a skilled potter. They had two sons, Jack and Warren. Unfortunately, Michael died in 1966 as a result of a fire in one of the kilns. When John Bird died in 1972, Michael's wife Jill, who had been working as sales manager, took over the business as managing director.

By that time the business was employing 20 people. She decided to create a limited company and raised capital to build a small factory on adjoining land. The factory produced moulded pots, which were

---

[1] The Glospot story, although based on an actual pottery in Gloucestershire, is purely imaginary, and the characters bear no relation to real people, living or dead.

cheaper than the hand-thrown ones and enabled the company to diversify into a wider market.

In 1990, Jack, her eldest son, who had been working his way up in the business, became production director. Two years later her second son, Warren, became marketing director. By 1995, when the story begins, Jill Bird is approaching 60 and is thinking of retirement.

The business has by now expanded considerably and is employing around 200 staff. The turnover is running at £2 million per annum. The company has weathered a number of setbacks, including the disastrous fire which destroyed the kiln and the moulding shop and killed Michael Bird. It also nearly went under in the recession at the end of the 1980s but managed to survive with a large bank loan. However, by 1993 the borrowing limit from the bank was reached and staff redundancies had occurred. The company was also facing other problems. The product line was beginning to lose its appeal with the public, who were favouring more colourful and artistic designs, which could be bought at very low prices from producers in developing countries.

As a result of the redundancies, there is now a feeling among the workforce that the management lacks inspiration and that the future of the company is uncertain. A number of skilled workers have left recently and got jobs in a newly opened car components factory in Cheltenham.

By far the biggest problem, however, is the rivalry of the two brothers for the succession to the managing directorship of the company. They know that their mother is thinking of retiring and has received an attractive offer from a Greek friend called Angelos to spend a major part of each year with him at his villa on the Greek island of Sifnos, where there are a number of interesting potteries. She has not designated a successor.

Jack is the elder. He has a solid track record—an engineering degree from Bristol University, an apprenticeship at Glospot and gradual promotion to his present position of responsibility for production. Warren, who is two years younger, has a more adventurous character and instead of studying at university, went to Australia to take up sheep farming with an uncle. This did not work out and he returned to the UK, where he worked as a salesperson for a company importing Japanese prints. Later he joined Glospot, where he learned the business and recently joined the board as marketing director. Jill has always preferred Warren, who is the more dynamic and forward looking of the two.

It is at this stage that Jill Bird has decided to call in a consultant. She wants someone who will take a look at the training policy of the company, improve morale and help the management to think creatively about the future. Ideally the consultant will also be able to do something about the bad relationship between her two sons. This is beginning to spread to a number of other staff, who are forming two camps, each supporting one of the brothers.

She had a number of candidates for the job of consultant, which she had advertised as possibly leading to a directorship if the consultancy role worked out satisfactorily. She had begun to realize the possibilities of human resource development and felt that the board needed strengthening with someone with this kind of expertise. The man she selected is called Tony Wakeman. He was not the most highly qualified, but he had an interesting background and a personality which she found attractive and impressive.

Tony had studied psychology at Durham University and then spent three years travelling around the world, during which time he had lived in India and California and worked in a pottery in Lesotho, South Africa. He had then returned to the UK and taken a job as public relations officer with a large national charity. In this capacity he had had to give frequent talks to the public and he realized that he had a natural gift for communication. He moved to a job as training officer with a company making moulded pottery in the Stoke area and studied for the Institute of Training and Development (as it was then) training diploma. He became very interested in a training method called Accelerated Learning, which seemed to have links with both India and California and which he found did a great deal to develop the potential of his trainees. His interest in accelerated learning led to his study of related methods and he had taken training in Neuro-Linguistic Programming, Brain Gym and the Alexander Technique.

In the first chapter, the story starts with Tony Wakeman arriving at Glospot and talking to Jill Bird. In a brief interview he explains the approach he plans to take in order to use what he calls 'The new learning' to explore the potential of the staff and to see what can be done to tap their creativity and improve their commitment to the company. Her unexpectedly brusque manner takes Tony aback and he wonders about underlying stress in the company.

In the second chapter, Tony Wakeman explains his concept of the role of a facilitator to Brian Downley, the conservative and sceptical technical training officer to the company. Tony senses resistance to change and a degree of resentment toward the senior management.

In the third chapter, Tony discusses with Brian Downley his reaction to some of the lessons on creative thinking and communication. Brian is becoming more receptive to Tony's ideas.

In Chapter 4, Tony works with Brian Downley on the first quadrant of a lesson. This covers preparation and the environment. He is appalled by the unwelcoming environment of the company's training room.

In Chapter 5, Tony works with Paul Toogood, the toolroom manager, in a joint lesson on safety. This is the second quadrant—the presentation stage.

In Chapter 6, Tony helps David Brooks, the kiln manager, to deliver a lesson teaching about a new glaze. This is the third quadrant—the primary activation or practice stage. He senses that David is not really interested in changing to a new glaze, but has been told to do so by Jack Bird, the production director.

In Chapter 7, Jill Bird meets with the managers and directors and leads a discussion about the responsibility of the company toward the community and the environment. This illustrates the fourth quadrant— the secondary activation or performance stage. She receives a hostile response from Jack, but is supported by Warren. The hostility between the two is uncomfortably obvious.

In Chapter 8, Tony discusses with a sceptical group of managers and directors how the brain works and how knowledge of their own thinking styles can help them to think more creatively, learn better and understand each other's points of view. At the end of the session Tony senses that there is the beginning of an attitude of cooperation among some of the managers who had been at loggerheads. However, the tension between the two brothers is tangible.

In Chapter 9, Tony finds the managers in a somewhat stressed condition and gives them a lesson in stress management. He succeeds in restoring a sense of calm by some physical and mental harmony exercises, accompanied by some Baroque music, illustrating the link between body and mind.

In Chapter 10, Tony illustrates the power of suggestion, when he addresses a group of nervous women, who have just joined the company, for training. A combination of attractive room decoration and a welcoming attitude makes them feel relaxed and looking forward to working with the company.

In Chapter 11, Tony talks about voice production and body movement. He explains to Roger Martin, the moulding shop manager, the importance of holding himself well and projecting his voice, when he gives a lesson about a new moulding machine to a group of moulding operatives. Roger is at first sceptical, but when he sees a video of himself he begins to take notice.

In Chapter 12, Tony talks to Warren Bird, the marketing director, about the need for Inner Awareness. When preparing a talk on product policy to the company's sales staff, Warren realizes that he has overlooked his own angry mood and that of the sales staff.

In Chapter 13, Tony has an important training session with the company's directors and managers on visualizing the future of the company. After preparation for the session with relaxation exercises, he gives them a guided visualization and an opportunity for individual reflection.

In Chapters 14 and 15, Tony talks about study skills to a group of trainees anxious to gain their NVQs in forming ceramic items. The trainees are excited about the new possibilities of learning opened up by the knowledge of their individual learning styles.

In Chapter 16, Tony Wakeman explains the creative process to the two brothers, Jack and Warren. They realize that this can be applied to the problem of the succession, as well as to the preparation of a training programme which will inspire the workforce.

In Chapter 17, Jill Bird looks back, with her friend Angelos from the island of Sifnos, on the outcome of the developments in the company leading up to her retirement. The seeds have been sown for the development of a learning organization.

Chronology of Glospot Ltd.

1890	John Bird born in Gloucester, of parents Jeremiah (a wool merchant) and Sarah, both Quakers
1914–1918	John Bird serves in ambulance unit in France
1919	John Bird starts apprenticeship with Elijah Beach in Wellington, Somerset
1926	John Bird rents derelict farm building outside Wychford, Gloucestershire and starts in business as a potter
1932	Two apprentices engaged
1934	John Bird marries Celia Westland, daughter of Cuthbert Westland, a surveyor
1935	Michael Bird born
1937	Mark Bird born
1953	Michael Bird joins Glospot and starts apprenticeship
1958	Michael Bird marries Jill Goodfellow (b. 1935), daughter of a potter from Northleach and herself a skilled potter
1959	Jack Bird born
1961	Warren Bird born
1966	Michael Bird killed in fire caused by explosion of a kiln in the pottery. This originated in an experiment with high temperature stoneware firing
1967	Jill Bird appointed as sales manager
1972	John Bird dies and is succeeded as managing director by Jill Bird
1973	Jill Bird forms pottery business into a limited company and raises capital to buy adjacent field and build a factory for moulded pots. Production of hand-thrown pots continues
1980	Jack Bird joins the company after taking a science degree at Bristol University
1982	Warren Bird joins the company after short career as a sheep farmer in Australia and as a salesperson for Japanese prints
1985	Sales reach £1 million per annum. Bank loan taken out to finance building of new moulding factory. Number of employees reaches 120
1989	Sales reach £2.2 million per annum. Number of employees now 200

1990	Jack Bird appointed as production director
1992	Warren Bird appointed as marketing director. Effects of recession are felt. Sales fall to £1.8 million. First redundancies declared
1993	Recession deepens. Bank loan of £200 000
1994	First big export order (from new chain of vegetarian restaurants in Russia)
1995	Sales rise to £2.1 million. Staff increased to 201

Organigram of Glospot Ltd.

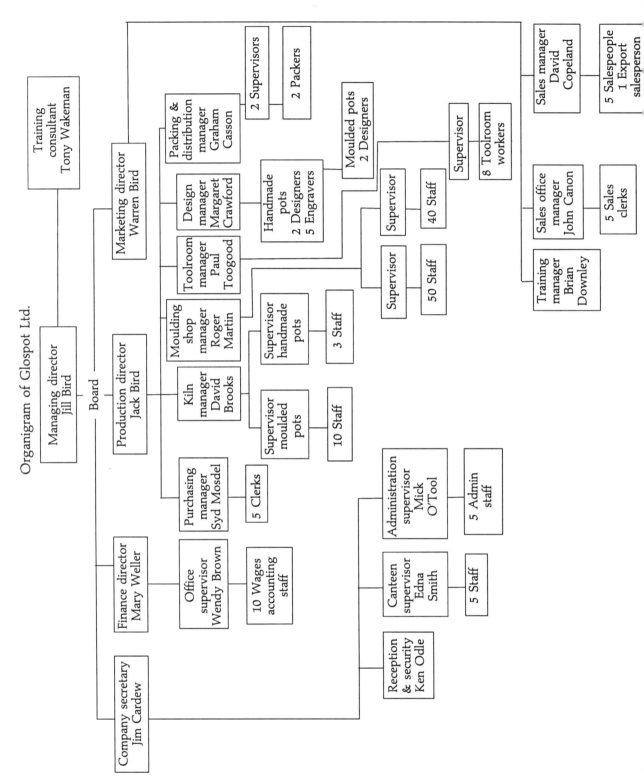

Figure I1.1 *Organigram of Glospot Ltd.*

PART 1

Fundamentals

1 A new approach to training

The greatest threat to any organization is not the lack of ability or resources, but the failure of imagination

David Meier

Scene *Jill Bird's office. Tony Wakeman has just arrived for his first day's work as training consultant with Glospot Ltd.*

'Sit down, Mr Wakeman,' said Jill Bird briskly. 'I haven't got much time. I'd like you to give me a run down on what it is you intend to do to stoke up some enthusiasm in this company. As I told you at your interview, we've had our share of problems recently. Morale is low. Standards are sloppy. Training is taking too long and not producing people who understand the job.'

'Well, you remember what I said at my interview about unused brain capacity?'

'We only use one per cent? I must say I find that incredible. But go on.'

'The figure isn't important, Mrs Bird. What is important is that everyone's brain is different. What I'd like to do first is to help everyone in the company to find out their thinking style. This will help people who are doing any kind of study. It may show too that there are some square pegs in round holes. And it may help people to get on with each other better.'

'What makes you think we're not getting on with each other?' asked Jill sharply. 'We're a family business, you know.'

'I didn't mean to imply that,' replied Tony, surprised at the vehemence of the interruption and wondering if he had touched a raw nerve. 'All I meant was that if people understand each other's thinking styles, they make allowances for differences of opinion. They begin to see them as sources of creative thinking.'

'All right. Point taken. What else have you in mind? You talked in your interview about a new approach to learning.'

'What I need to do is to try to find out why morale is low and to restore *enthusiasm for the job and for learning about new developments. One of the basic features of the new approach I spoke about is the activation of the emotional part of the brain—the limbic system.'*

'Be careful how you go, Mr Wakeman. This is a very conservative company. Our people don't take kindly to touchy–feely ideas.'

'I'll bear that in mind, Mrs Bird. But I don't expect they'll object to being reminded that they have bodies and that these need to be respected if they're going to work and learn efficiently.'

'No. But we don't want compulsory physical jerks or the company song three times a day. I'm sorry, but I can hear the visitor I'm expecting just arriving. We'll have to finish this conversation later. You'd better get started as quickly as possible. But don't tread on any toes, please.'

The handshake Jill offered Tony was perfunctory. She was already searching hastily through the pile of papers on her desk in preparation for her visitor.

As already outlined in the Preface, a number of recent discoveries about the human brain have had an important impact on the theories about learning and teaching. The following are some further comments on the eight discoveries about the brain which have a direct bearing on training.

Brain capacity

There are approximately one trillion (1 000 000 000 000) neurons (nerve cells) in the human brain, each one capable of storing information and of making contact with between a thousand and a hundred thousand other cells.[1] The number of combinations which they can make with each other is virtually limitless, greater, it is said, than the number of atoms in the universe. The whole of the world's telephone system is equivalent to only about one gram of the brain, the same size as a pea.[2] The storage capacity of the brain is sufficient to record a thousand new bits of information every second from birth to old age. We use well under ten per cent of this capacity, probably more like one per cent or even 0.1 per cent for many people.[3] This means that there is an enormous amount of untapped potential in the people who make up organizations—potential for creative thinking, problem solving and learning. If you as a trainer are constantly aware of this you can regard each training session as an opportunity to help participants to get in touch with their unused brain capacity (see Chapter 8).

Barriers

The development of brain potential is restricted by limiting beliefs. These may be the result of the cultural norms of society or of the early childhood conditioning of the individual. These limiting beliefs are barriers which are difficult if not impossible to overcome on the conscious level. However, they can be reduced or eliminated if the approach is subconscious. Suggestion is the means of achieving this.[4] As a facilitator you can do much through the use of body language, tone of voice and appropriate language to overcome limiting beliefs on the part of learners. The environment and the group dynamic can be powerful additional means (see Chapters 4 and 10).

Right and left brain

It is now a well-known fact that the cerebral cortex consists of two hemispheres.[5] The left hemisphere deals with information in a logical, analytical and linear fashion. The right hemisphere tends to see patterns and wholes and to be attracted by colour, art and music. It is imaginative and intuitive. Most people have a natural preference to think with one side rather than the other. They are said to be left- or right-brain dominant.

The significance of brain dominance for trainers is that lessons have to be prepared and delivered in a way which makes it possible for both right- and left-brain dominant participants to learn easily. For this reason it is important that you as a trainer are aware of your own dominance. If you are not, it will be difficult for you to realize that your own way of presenting a subject may be at variance with the preferred way of learning of some of the group members. Every lesson needs to have left brain elements (logical, analytical, sequential) and right brain elements (global, emotional, artistic, inter-personal) (see Chapter 8). Another aspect of brain dominance is that people can be helped by appropriate activities to develop the non-dominant side of their brain. This enables them to gain access to some of the untapped potential of their brain. They can learn to be more creative and imaginative if they are left-brain dominant or more logical and rational in their thinking and behaviour if they are right-brain dominant.

The limbic system

The limbic system is part of the mid-brain, situated below the cerebral cortex.[6] It is also known as the mammalian brain, because it shares with other mammals unthinking emotional responses, such as love and hate, confidence and fear, like and dislike. It acts as a kind of gatekeeper or monitor on incoming information. It will only allow this information to pass into the long-term memory if it contains some pleasant emotional content. Extremely unpleasant emotional experiences are also allowed to pass through, but they are often repressed below the conscious level.

The monitoring role of the limbic system means that much of what you teach will not be remembered unless it has some kind of emotional content. This means that your lessons should contain activities which are enjoyable and entertaining as well as being purely informative.

A dialogue is a good way of introducing a subject, as it brings in a human element. Music, role play, puppets play, creative thinking exercises, and visualization are other ways of engaging positive emotions and ensuring that the limbic system acts as a help and not a hindrance to learning (see Chapter 8).

Sensory modalities

One of the important contributions to the theory of learning made by Neuro-Linguistic Programming (NLP) is that people learn and think with a preference for a particular sense or combination of senses.[7] Some people prefer to process information visually. If they are learning something, they like to see it written or illustrated. They are visual learners. Others may like to hear it. They like lectures and verbal explanations. They are auditory learners. A third group prefer to have some active physical involvement with the new information. They are kinesthetic learners. As a trainer you should always bear in mind the different learning preferences of the people you are teaching. In every group there will be people who prefer to see information written down or displayed visually. So the key points of the lesson should be reinforced by the use of OHP slides, flip charts or posters. There will be auditory learners, who will be happy to listen to you talk. You can help them further by providing them with back-up cassettes for revision, by the use of music and by the way you use your voice. There will also be a number of people who must have some form of physical activity if they are to respond positively to your lesson. So you need to make sure that every lesson contains some periods of physical activity, linked, if possible, to the subject being taught. Brain Gym exercises can be used to help everyone with the learning of any subject and provide the opportunity of satisfying the needs of kinesthetic learners (see Chapter 8).

Visualization

It is now believed that the brain uses the same neurological pathways to record memories of a visualized activity as it uses for an actual physical one. A clear multi-sensory visualization of a coming event, be it a marathon run or a public speech, can act as an effective rehearsal and powerful source of confidence and motivation.

Athletes and an increasing number of high performers in other fields are becoming increasingly aware of the power of visualization to help them achieve their goals. You can assist your course participants to develop their untapped potential by teaching them the skill of visualization. It can be used in many ways—for creative thinking and problem solving, for memorization, for goal setting, for stress management and for inter-personal relationships, to mention just a few.[8]

Some people may find it difficult to create mental images, particularly if their thinking style is dominantly auditory or kinesthetic. You can help them to become visualizers by getting them first to create a mental image in one of the other sensory modes and then linking it to a visual image. There are a number of simple exercises which can help people who are blocked to realize that they can visualize (see Chapter 13).

The body–mind link

It is now widely accepted by the medical and educational professions that stress inhibits learning. People learn best when they are in a state of relaxed awareness and do not feel threatened or anxious. Experiments carried out by Georgi Lozanov, a medical doctor and psychiatrist practising in Bulgaria in the 1960s, showed that people could learn a language at least three times faster in a relaxed state than when they were in the stressed conditions of a normal classroom.[9]

Further research carried out by Dr Paul Dennison in the United States showed that certain parts of the brain can be activated to perform particular types of activity at an optimum level. These include study skills such as reading, writing, thinking creatively or carrying out motor skill activities such as keyboard operation. The activation is carried out by a range of physical movements known as Brain Gym.[10] They also have the effect of raising energy. In the classroom you have an ideal opportunity of helping your learners to realize the importance of bringing the body into the learning process. You can teach them skills which they can use when they are studying on their own and which can enhance considerably their general well-being and their ability to use their brains effectively. In addition to the two methods mentioned above, there is a whole range of exercises from Office Yoga,[11] Autogenic Training[12] and the Alexander Technique[13] which can be used as and when appropriate (see Chapter 9).

Multiple intelligences

Professor Howard Gardner of Harvard University has challenged the assumption that intelligence can be measured only by the traditional tests of linguistic or mathematical/logical ability. In his *Frames of Mind*[14] he describes five other intelligences which are equally valid and useful in the right circumstances. They are visual/spatial, kinesthetic, inter-personal, intra-personal and musical.

You can use the concept of multiple intelligences to enliven and enrich any lesson and to give all the participants an opportunity of working with their most highly developed intelligence. For example you can arrange small-group activities to address the inter-personal intelligence, visualizations for the intra-personal, problem solving for the logical/ mathematical and creative writing assignments for the linguistic intelligence. This enhances self-esteem and draws on the resources available within the group.

Notes and references

1 Gilling, D. and Brightwell, R. (1982) *The Human Brain* (p. 13), Orbis Publications and the BBC, London.
Dryden, G. and Voss, J. (1993) *The Learning Revolution* (Chapter 3), Profile Books, New Zealand.
Buzan, T. (1974) *Use Your Head* (p. 17), BBC Books, London.

2 Russell, P. (1984) *The Brain Book* (p. 7), Routledge & Kegan Paul, London.

3 Ibid.

4 Lozanov, G. (1978) *Suggestology and Outlines of Suggestopody* (Chapter 4), Gordon and Breach Science Publishers, London.

5 Gilling, D. and Brightwell, R., op. cit. (pp. 10–11).
Russell, P. op. cit. (Chapter 4).

6 (Six editorial consultants) (1982) *The Brain—A User's Manual* (pp. 40 and 41), New English Library, Sevenoaks, Kent.

7 O'Connor, J. and Seymour, J. (1993) *Introducing Neuro-Linguistic Programming* (Chapter 2), Aquarian Press, Wellingborough.

8 Bandler, R. (1985) *Using Your Brain—For a Change* (Chapter 1), real People Press, Moab, Utah USA.
Gallwey, T. (1974) *The Inner Game of Tennis* (pp. 157–178), Bantam Books, London.

9 Lozanov, G. op. cit. (Chapter 5).

10 Dennison, P. and Dennison, G. (1994) *Brain Gym for Business—Instant Brain Boosters for On-the-Job Success*, Edu-Kinesthetics Inc., Ventura, California.

11 Friedberger, J. (1991) *Office Yoga*, Thorsons Publishing Group, Wellingborough.

12 Kermani, K. (1990) *Autogenic Training*, Souvenir Press, London.

13 Hodgkinson, L. and Piatkus, J. (1988) *The Alexander Technique and how it can help you*, Piatkus Books, London.

14 Gardner, H. (1983) *Frames of Mind—The Theory of Multiple Intelligences*, Paladin, London.

Mind map for Chapter 1—the Brain

2 Creative facilitation

Significant learning combines the logical and the intuitive, the intellect and the feelings, the concept and the experience, the idea and the meaning. When we learn in that way, we are whole, utilizing all our masculine and feminine capacities.

Carl Rogers *Freedom to Learn*

Scene *The office of Brian Downley, the technical training officer of Glospot Ltd. Tony Wakeman was talking to him about the concept of facilitation.*

'You've mentioned this word "facilitation" several times, Tony. I'm not sure what it really means.' *The tone of Brian Downley's voice was disgruntled. He was clearly suspicious of this newcomer who had been foisted on him.*

'Well, it's another way of looking at training, really,' *replied Tony, searching for some common ground with this experienced and sceptical older man, who had spent his whole life working at Glospot, first making pots and then training others to make them.*

'The word really means making it easy for people to learn, to help them forward. It means providing opportunities to learn, rather than just teaching. It means encouraging and supporting individuals and helping them to find their natural way of learning. It means gradually handing over the learning process to the group. It's about empowering people to believe in themselves and to become active, rather than passive, learners.'

'Been in this business long, have you?' *The sneer in the older man's voice was unmistakeable. Tony realized that he had a problem on his hands and it was not just one of communication.*

'No,' *he replied evenly.* 'I was training manager at Capital Ceramics for three years. And I've worked in a pottery in South Africa. But I realize I've had nothing like the experience you've had. I've got a lot to learn from you. But ideas about training and how people learn have changed a bit over the past few years. It's because we know a bit more about how the brain works. I'm *very willing to share some of the ideas with you. Together we might be able to do something to help the company get on its feet.'*

'What do you mean, hand over the learning process to the group? Our job is to train them, not sit back and watch them make mistakes.' His voice was gruff, but Brian was now looking at Tony instead of avoiding his eyes.

'Well, it's a matter of having trust, I suppose,' replied Tony. 'Obviously you've got to start by telling them what to do. But gradually you can get a group of learners to share the responsibility for what goes on. And in the end you can more or less step back and be there as a kind of resource if they need you. It means doing a lot of listening and a lot of observing—and knowing how and when to step in if necessary. It's not all that easy. But it usually produces better long-term results—because it teaches people to stand on their own feet. And you get a lot more commitment and maybe some useful ideas.'

'Perhaps you'd better find out a bit more about what's going on in this company before you start any of these new ideas of yours,' replied Brian darkly.

Tony thought it wisest to let the matter drop for the moment. He wondered what lay behind Brian's last remark.

As Tony Wakeman said, facilitation means making it easy for people to learn. The word comes from the Latin *facilis*, meaning 'to make easy'. However, as we have mentioned in the introduction, it is about more than that. It is about the empowering and transformation of individuals, so that they can widen their horizons, set and achieve their own goals and realize their potential.

Paradoxically, however, this means becoming aware that as a trainer you are in a position of immense influence and power. Within the micro-world of your classroom, every word that you say and how you say it will have an effect. Every gesture you make will be registered. The way you move and hold your body will speak as loudly as your voice and transmit an even more powerful message. And the environment you have created in the classroom will exercise an influence throughout the lesson. You are like a director/actor performing a one-man show, which you have scripted and stage managed yourself. We are talking here about the power of suggestion. This is a basic aspect of the work of Dr Lozanov and it is described more fully in Chapter 10. In Chapter 11 you will find some guidance about how to use your body and your voice to communicate effectively in the classroom.

This may seem a daunting prospect, but the metaphor of the actor on stage should not give you stage fright. It is rather to persuade you to think of each lesson that you give as being a unique performance with potentially far-reaching effects on your audience. It is only if you think of it in this way that you will rise to the challenge which being a creative trainer represents. Being a trainer who is truly creative offers the prospect of an immensely satisfying and fulfilling vocation. Just as the artist and the writer achieve fulfilment through bringing creativity to their work, so can a trainer. Each lesson becomes an opportunity for producing a creative act and for making a difference in the lives of other people.

Making a difference is perhaps the bottom line of the trainer's balance sheet of values. To make a difference for the better in the life of another person can give more real satisfaction than even the highest financial reward.

The audience

Unlike the stage performer, and indeed some traditional trainers, the creative trainer is acutely aware of her audience. She realizes that each participant has an individual learning style and that the lesson needs to be designed so as to make it easy for each individual to learn in the style which suits them best. She will make sure that the lesson contains both visual and auditory elements and opportunities for physical involvement. She will realize that to be successful the lesson must contain human interest and have an appeal to the emotional part of the brain, the limbic system. This is described in Chapter 8, How the brain works.

Atmosphere

The creative trainer will bear in mind that the learning she wants to take place can only happen if there is an atmosphere of relaxation and mutual trust. She will take responsibility for doing what is needed to create this atmosphere. Some suggestions for this are described under the heading 'Group dynamic' in Chapter 6.

The body and energy levels

This trainer will take into account the important and much neglected fact that the body plays a vital part in learning. She will maintain energy in the group at an optimum level by the regular introduction of exercises from Brain Gym, Office Yoga and other sources. She will make sure that windows are opened from time to time and that everyone has an opportunity of breathing deeply. She will introduce relaxation exercises when appropriate. Only in these ways can the brains of the participants be kept alert and receptive. Chapter 9 gives suggestions for this kind of activity.

Visualization

She will be aware of the power of visualization in enhancing self image, in achieving goals and in stimulating the imagination. She will use guided imagery in the lesson and she will show her learners how they can use it as a tool for personal development. In Chapter 13 you will find some hints on how to use visualization in both these ways.

Inner awareness

The potentially creative trainer will recognize the crucial role of inner awareness in her progress towards her goal. This means taking the time to check out her feelings before she enters the classroom and taking steps to ensure that her emotional state is such that it is going to create the right atmosphere in the group. It means being aware of her preferred thinking style and adjusting her lesson to take account of the diversity of thinking styles in the group. It means being continually alert to what is going on below the surface among the members of the group and if necessary bringing it out into the open. This is dealt with in Chapter 13.

Learner-centred orientation

What all this means is that the creative trainer must be capable of shifting the focus away from herself and from the content of the lesson to the learners and their perceptions. In other words, she must know how to adopt a learner-centred orientation. This is not to say that she must forget her own role and the content of what she is teaching. It means that she must have the skill of shifting view points when necessary. She will be able to visualize herself in the classroom and mentally rehearse her words and actions. She will imagine herself stepping inside the body of one or more of the participants and looking at herself from that person's point of view. Then she will disassociate herself mentally from both the learner and herself and look at the progress of the lesson from the point of view of an outside observer.

Rapport

Another skill which the creative trainer needs to cultivate is that of rapport. Even her best lesson will not be fully effective unless she has established good personal relations with the individual members of the group. She needs to know how to pick up on the mood of a group from the body language of its members, to 'match'[1] it and then if necessary 'lead' the group into a more appropriate state for learning. She will know how to use breaks and informal opportunities to create rapport with individual members, particularly anyone who seems to be having difficulties with learning or who seems to have personal problems. These skills are part of Neuro-Linguistic Programming and can only be referred to briefly in a book of this length. Taking a course in NLP is the only way to acquire them at a deep level and is highly recommended.[2]

Figure 2.1   ... *she needs to pick up the mood of a group from the body language of the members ...*

Technology

Finally, a word about technology. The creative trainer will not be averse to using the ever-more sophisticated equipment which is available to make learning more effective. On occasion she may well choose to use an overhead projector, a video recorder, a video camera, a 35mm projector or a CD ROM disk. But she will be aware that there is a price to pay in handing over her role as facilitator to a mechanical or electronic substitute. This price is the interruption of the personal rapport which has been established in her communication with the group. It is almost as if the director of an orchestra suddenly steps down from the podium and puts a mechanical, life-sized puppet in his place. The puppet might conceivably be able to keep the orchestra in time, but the players will immediately feel the lack of the personality and charisma of the director. Furthermore they will feel unacknowledged as individuals.

So the creative trainer will be aware that her creativity and rapport with the group is under threat if she relies too much on technology. No matter how many well-prepared slides she may have to show, she should resist the temptation to allow them to become the main focus of the lesson. The glazed eyes and slumped bodies of the participants will tell her when it is time to switch off the overhead projector and step on stage again herself.

In the next chapter you will see how the trainer's role gradually changes from 'hierarchical', when she takes full charge of what goes on in the classroom, through 'cooperative', when she hands over some of the responsibility to the group, to 'autonomous', when the group makes most of its own decisions and she becomes more of a coach or advisor.

Notes and references

1 'Matching' is an NLP term meaning creating rapport with another person by mirroring in a discreet way some of the ways in which they are using their body, such as their posture, gestures and breathing. For further information, see O'Connor, J. and Seymour, J. (1993) *Introducing Neuro-Linguistic Programming* (pp. 18–23), Aquarian Press, Wellingborough.
2 Details of NLP courses available in the UK can be obtained from the Association of Neuro-Linguistic Programming, 48 Corser Street, Stourbridge, West Midlands DY8 2DQ (Tel: 01384 443935).

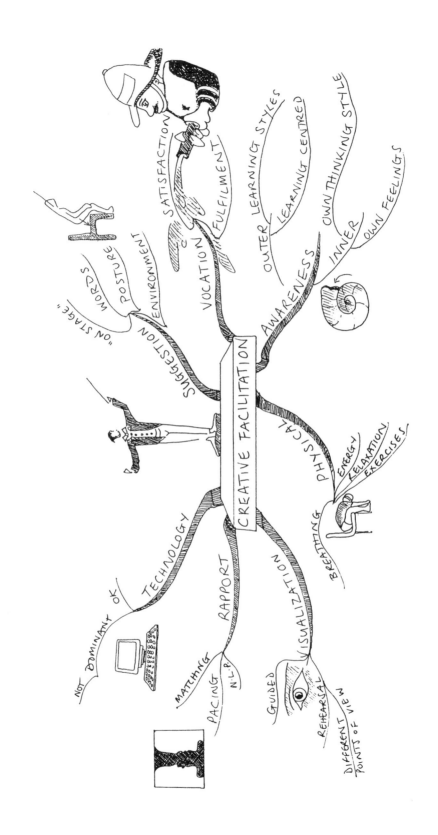

Mind map for Chapter 2—creative facilitation

PART 2

Building a training course

3 The four-quadrant teaching cycle—An overview

In our present educational system, the attention given to the right brain is minimal compared to the training lavished on the left side

Roger Sperry

Scene *Tony Wakeman's temporary office. It was three weeks later and Tony was discussing with Brian Downley his reaction to some of the lessons on creative thinking and communication which Tony has been giving to the managers and supervisors of the company.*

'So you don't feel happy about the new training programme,' said Tony, leaning back in his chair, arms folded.

'There's a lot of things I don't rightly understand about it,' replied Brian. 'Some things I agree with. For instance, I think it's a good idea to write to people in advance and tell them a bit about the course. I agree too that I should give them the big picture at the beginning of the lesson. But I can't see anything wrong with presenting information with an overhead projector. They've always learned that way in the past. I give them an opportunity to ask questions. And I give them handouts at the end. I can't see the need for all this going on about the classroom environment, acting out dialogues and getting them to play games. It seems a waste of time to me.'

'I understand your concern about wasting time,' replied Tony. 'But the fact is that the method I am proposing actually saves time. This is because it's designed to appeal to individual learning styles. And it's learner centred, not teacher centred. So trainees learn by doing and experiencing, not just by passive listening.'

'Right. But I don't feel happy with all this play acting.'

'I can understand that. But there's a reason for that, too. Take the playlet I usually perform at the beginning. What this does is to introduce some human interest into the lesson. If you want to engage the whole brain, including the *part which responds to emotional content, you need to bring in something to interest it. So this is why I give the participants a bit of drama and humour at the beginning. The same applies when I give them roles or get them to play games. They begin to enjoy it. They get actively involved. They can be creative.'*

'That seems to make sense. But I'd like to know how it all fits together.'

'Right. First of all you need to decide on how much control you are going to take over what the group does. Are you going to make all the decisions yourself? Are you going to cooperate with the group in deciding how learning is to take place? Or are you going to let them decide how they are going to learn—in other words, are you going to give them autonomy? You may of course decide to move gradually from one kind of facilitating to another. That's probably the best way. You need to be fairly directive at the beginning and then gradually hand over the learning process to the group. I find it useful to divide the process into four quadrants. Perhaps I can explain it better by drawing it on a flip chart . . .'

The creative trainer four-quadrant teaching cycle is described in outline below and in detail in the following four chapters. First of all, however, here are some general considerations. Before starting to prepare any lesson or course it is important to decide what your teaching style is going to be. You will be likely to act in one of the following three modes:

1 **The hierarchical mode**. Directing the learning process yourself.
2 **The cooperative mode**. Sharing your power over the learning process with the group.
3 **The autonomous mode**. Giving the group freedom to find their own way.

These three modes are described in John Heron's *The Facilitator's Handbook*.[1] Heron's book is mainly about these three modes and how they relate to what he calls the six dimensions of facilitation. These are:

1 **The planning dimension**. This concerns establishing goals for the group and the planning necessary to achieve them.
2 **The meaning dimension**. This is the factual content of the course— what you want the trainees to learn.
3 **The confronting dimension**. There will in most groups be undercurrents of resistance to learning and to willing cooperation between members. These issues need to be raised to the conscious level and addressed if the group is to function harmoniously.
4 **The feeling dimension**. This is the affective aspect of facilitation. As mentioned in the conversation at the beginning of the chapter, feelings play an important part in the learning process. The facilitator's role is to recognize this and to use feelings to help and not hinder learning.

5 **The structuring dimension**. This has to do with methods of learning. Decisions need to be taken about timing, equipment, handouts, group activities, etc.
6 **The valuing dimension**. This is about creating an atmosphere in which every member of the group feels respected and valued.

Each one of these dimensions can be approached in one of the three facilitating modes—hierarchical, cooperative or autonomous. This means that there are 18 basic options (see pp. 23–25 and Chapters 3–8 of *The Facilitator's Handbook* by John Heron). Let us see now how this approach relates to the four quadrants.

Quadrant 1 Preparation

This quadrant covers all the things you do before the lesson actually starts and it relates to Heron's Planning dimension. The more time and attention you give it the more likely it is that the lesson will succeed.

Figure 3.1   ... *there will in any group be undercurrents of resistance to learning and to willing cooperation between members* ...

At this stage it is worth giving attention to creating the right mental 'state'. This corresponds to Heron's Valuing and Feeling dimensions and needs to be thought about and prepared. The following are some of the things you can do to create the right mental state in your trainees:

- **Advance communication**. Expectations are raised and fears allayed.
- **Environment**. Seating is designed to promote group interaction (usually in a circle or horseshoe). Posters are placed on the walls to reinforce information and to bring in an artistic dimension. Music may be used if appropriate.
- **Welcoming atmosphere**. The facilitator welcomes participants and gets to know their names as soon as possible.
- **Positive mood**. Mistakes are not criticized but regarded as valuable feedback. This is explained at the beginning and emphasized by a written reminder in the form of a poster.
- **Establishment of rapport**. Between the facilitator and the group and between the members of the group.
- **Attention to individuals**. Goals, needs and concerns are addressed.

They are described in more detail in Chapter 4.

Quadrant 2 Presentation

This is the presentation stage and it corresponds to Heron's Meaning and Structuring dimensions. It is likely that it will be mainly in the hierarchical mode, with you as the facilitator directing operations. It is important to bear in mind that the presentation should be made in such a way as to address as many different learning styles as possible. This means incorporating some or all of the following elements: visual; auditory; kinesthetic/physical; logical/analytical/linear (left-brain dominant); global (right-brain dominant).

After establishing rapport, as described in Quadrant 1, you should normally give an overview of the lesson, making clear the aims and what the trainees will be able to do at the end. This information should be conveyed verbally and visually (OHP or flip chart). Connections should be made with their jobs or personal development aims, so that trainees can see 'what's in it for them'.

It is often useful then to put participants into small groups and to discuss what they already know about the subject. Each group can prepare a mind map and then share their findings with the whole group. A group mind map can then be prepared on a flip chart.

The presentation itself can take a number of forms, for example:

- A dialogue acted out by the facilitator and a colleague or member of the group
- A dialogue presented by the facilitator with glove puppets
- A dialogue acted out by the facilitator with an imaginary partner
- A soliloquy performed by the facilitator

- Giving a concert reading, i.e. reading a dialogue or text with a background of Baroque music
- Telling a story, either factual or metaphorical
- Making a challenging statement
- Playing a video or audio tape
- Involving the group with lists—for example, getting sub-groups to prepare checklists of how to design a course
- Using visualization—guided, semi-guided or unguided

It may, of course, be appropriate at certain times to use an OHP or flip chart to present information visually as well as orally. In this case the visual information should be made as interesting as possible, using colours and illustrations. There should not be too much information on an OHP foil. It is usually unwise to project pages from a book; the print is usually too small to be read easily and there is too much information to be absorbed at once. It is better to write key words and to explain them orally.

Quadrant 3 Practice

This is the primary activation stage and it corresponds to a further development of Heron's Meaning, Structuring, Feeling and Valuing dimensions. As part of this development, you may begin to move from the hierarchical to the cooperative mode, inviting trainees to join with you in making decisions regarding activities. Occasional supportive use of the Confronting dimension may be appropriate to raise consciousness in the trainees of any blocks to this more active and self-directed learning.

There are many activations which can be carried out at this stage and a number are described in Chapter 6. They include: games, skits, role plays, mnemonics for helping memory, mind maps and discussions. This is an opportunity to involve as many learning styles as possible and to give trainees a chance to use one or more of the seven intelligences described in Chapter 8. To recapitulate, these are: linguistic, logical/mathematical, spatial, musical, kinesthetic, inter-personal and intra-personal.

You might find it useful at the end of this stage (or indeed at the end of Quadrants 2 or 4) to give a review concert; that is to read a summary of the lesson with a background of Baroque music, with the trainees in a relaxed state (see Chapter 5).

Quadrant 4 Performance

This is the secondary activation stage. It continues to develop the Heron dimensions mentioned in Quadrant 3, but the mode may now be more autonomous. In other words, you hand over much of the structuring of the learning activities to the trainees to decide entirely on their own. However, it is at this stage that personal differences and antagonisms may become more apparent, so your role as facilitator may still be important, including supportive use of the Confronting dimension. You can also take the opportunity to build-up self-esteem and confidence in the participants—an important aspect of Heron's Valuing dimension. Your feedback on their autonomous group work and presentations can be an important part of this process.

Testing, evaluation and feedback are usually carried out at this stage. They may take the form of activities similar to the ones already described. Some of the activities might be:

- Demonstration of knowledge
- Team games which challenge knowledge
- Unguided visualizations
- Trainees teaching each other
- Comparison of individual mind maps
- Informal testing
- Review
- Evaluation
- Field work

There should at the end of each lesson be some kind of closing ritual. This is particularly important at the end of a course, when a group has worked closely over a period of time and will not be meeting again as a group.

Notes and references

1 Heron, J. (1989) *The Facilitator's Handbook* (pp. 16–20), Kogan Page, London. John Heron facilitates workshops internationally. His address is: Podere Gello, San Cipriano, 56048 Volterra (Pi), Tuscany, Italy.

Mind map for Chapter 3—four quadrant cycle

FOUR QUADRANT CYCLE

1ST PREPARATION (PLANNING)
- ADVANCE COMMUNICATION
- INDIVIDUAL GOALS
- ENVIRONMENT
- WELCOMING ATMOSPHERE
- POSITIVE MOOD
- RAPPORT

2ND PRESENTATION (MEANING & STRUCTURE)
- LEARNING STYLES VISUAL AUDITORY KINESTHETIC
- LEFT BRAIN RIGHT BRAIN
- OVERVIEW
- CONNECT WITH AIMS
- WHAT THEY ALREADY KNOW
- DIALOGUES/STORIES
- VISUALIZATIONS
- VIDEO CLIPS
- O.H.P.
- FLIPCHART
- COLOUR

3RD PRACTICE (CONFRONTING MEANING STRUCTURING FEELING VALUING)
- REVIEW CONCEPT
- 7 INTELLIGENCES
- DISCUSSIONS
- MNEMONICS MINDMAPS
- ROLE PLAYS
- GAMES SKITS

4TH PERFORMANCE (VALUING CONFRONTING)
- DEMONSTRATION OF KNOWLEDGE
- TEAM GAMES
- PAIR TEACHING
- FIELD WORK
- INFORMAL TESTING
- CLOSING RITUAL

DIMENSIONS
- PLANNING
- MEANING
- CONFRONTING
- FEELING
- STRUCTURING
- VALUING

MODES
- CO-OPERATIVE
- AUTONOMOUS
- HIERARCHICAL

25

4 Quadrant 1—Preparation

When a facilitator creates, even to a modest degree, a classroom climate characterised by all that she can achieve of realness, prizing and empathy, when she trusts the constructive tendency of the individual and the group; then she discovers that she has inaugurated an educational revolution

Carl Rogers *Freedom to Learn*

Scene *The training room used by Brian Downley, the technical training officer. As Tony looked around he realized how little of what he had said to Brian about his new approach to training had actually been understood. He looked at the boxes stacked in the corner, the litter on the floor and the unemptied ashtrays on the tables. He took in the rows of desks and hard seats, the brown walls and the flickering fluorescent light tubes on the ceiling. He turned to Brian, who was standing beside him looking somewhat uneasy as he watched Tony's reaction to his training room.*

'Brian' he said. 'How do you feel about working in this room? You were telling me yesterday how tired you've been feeling. Could it have anything to do with the environment you're working in?'

'Well, I agree it's not exactly ideal,' replied Brian defensively. 'But this is what the company has given me.'

'Just sit down for a minute,' said Tony. 'Would you be willing to carry out a short experiment in creative thinking?'

'Okay. If you think we've got time for that sort of thing. I've got a class starting in an hour.'

'This won't take more than twenty minutes,' replied Tony. 'I'd like you to sit down and make yourself as comfortable as you can on one of these chairs. Close your eyes, stretch your arms over your head and take a few deep breaths. Relax your arms and legs. Imagine that they are becoming quite heavy . . .

Imagine now that you are floating out of your chair and up through the ceiling, so that you are looking down on the building from a considerable height ... Now imagine that you are flying through the air and that you arrive at a part of the country that you have never visited before. The landscape is very beautiful. You can see green fields, woods, houses with attractive gardens and picturesque villages ...

Take time to fill in the details for yourself. You notice that one of the buildings is a purpose-built training centre. You float down to it, through the roof and into a room where a training session is in progress. It is one of the most attractive rooms that you have ever seen. Notice the pastel shades of the walls, the colourful pictures and posters, the soft lights, the thick carpet and the way the comfortable chairs are arranged in a circle. Look at the expression of lively interest on the faces of the participants. How do you feel in this room? How do you think the course participants are feeling? How would you feel if you worked in an environment like this?'

As mentioned in Chapter 3, the first quadrant of the training cycle is concerned with creating an appropriate mental state in the course participants. A seed will only germinate and grow if it is planted in well-prepared, fertile ground. In the same way new ideas will only become established in the minds of learners if they are in a receptive mood, if the learning environment is pleasant and if the relationships in the group are cooperative and non-threatening. To achieve this, attention should be given to the following matters:

1 Preparing the learner for the learning event.
2 Preparing a welcoming learning environment.
3 Connecting and engaging with the learners and building a collaborative learning environment.

Preparing the learner for the learning event

Joining instructions offer a good opportunity for the trainer to start creating in the minds of the course participants a positive attitude towards the training event. Very often joining instructions are cursory and purely factual. They do little if anything to arouse interest or a sense of anticipation.

Here are some ideas for preparing more imaginative joining instructions:

- Use coloured paper
- Summarize in the form of a mind map, possibly in colour
- Prepare a puzzle, which the recipient has to put together to understand the instructions. This might fit in with the theme of the course, for example problem-solving
- Send a computer disk with simple instructions on performing some computer program concept (for a computer course)

- Record the instructions on an audio tape. The tape could include testimonials from previous participants and perhaps recorded extracts from a course. A video tape could also be used for this purpose

This is by no means an exhaustive list and you may well think of other ideas to make your joining instructions more interesting. The aim is to produce a positive state of mind in the participants towards the course and the material they will be learning.

Creating a positive learning environment

As you will have read in Chapter 3, the environment plays an important part in suggestion, which is at the heart of Dr Lozanov's theory and forms the basis of Accelerated Learning. A warm, welcoming environment can go a long way towards overcoming some of the logical, critical barriers which people use to protect themselves, but which can prevent learning.

The following is a checklist of some of the ways in which an environment can be created which will enhance learning:

Room layout

The first question to settle is whether the participants should be provided with tables. These are obviously helpful to write and put books on. But they can seriously interfere with physical activities which may be important for the group dynamic or for allowing kinesthetic learners to become involved. Books can be put on the floor and knees can be used for writing notes. This makes it possible for the seats to be arranged in either horseshoe or circular formation. In this form of seating there are no physical barriers; people are open to each other and it is possible to get up and move around easily.

If, however, it is felt that tables are essential, then they can be arranged in such a way as to promote group interaction. Arranging them in clusters in what is sometimes known as 'cabaret style' allows small groups of say four or five to socialize and work together. This induces a feeling of collaboration and reduces stress.

Colour

One of the most effective ways of stimulating the right brain is the use of colour. Colourful rooms invite interest and curiosity and appeal to the emotions. Ideally the walls should be painted in attractive pastel colours, but this is rarely within a trainer's power. However, colour can be added in a variety of ways, for example by the use of posters, pictures or peripheral wall charts and messages. Colour can also be added to OHP slides and handouts.

Music

Music can help to reduce stress and anxiety and it adds another sensory dimension to the room. It can make periods of silent reflection more acceptable and thinking more creative. It can turn a cold, empty environment into a place where people feel warm and secure. It can raise energy and produce a state of relaxed awareness which is ideal for receptive learning. Music that is especially suitable for creating a state of relaxed awareness is Baroque. Some of this kind of music, written between about 1600 and 1750, mainly the largo and adagio passages, has a beat of around 60 to the minute, which corresponds to the beat of the human heart when the body is relaxed and at rest. It is used extensively in the teaching of languages, when long dialogues are read by the teacher in so-called 'concert sessions'. It can also be used by trainers, particularly for reviewing material at the end of the day.

In a survey carried out among 156 trainers in Germany by the SKILL Institute in Heidelberg,[1] the following results were obtained:

| Aim | Rank in order of preference | | | | |
	1st	2nd	3rd	4th	5th
Creates a good learning environment	106	27	8	2	0
Makes teaching more holistic by appealing to several senses	48	27	26	7	6
Improves the performance of my participants	30	21	24	13	6
Makes me feel good	19	17	16	25	12
Brings more rhythm into my teaching	9	3	13	13	18

Comments from the trainers included the following:

'Relationships within the group were more free and easy.'

'At first I was anxious, but also curious, about trying music—but then I was amazed by its effect.'

'Expectation, receptivity and concentration have all improved.'

'Music calms or energizes, depending on the need.'

'I feel good when I hear music.'

'The attitude of the learners to the learning material is improved.'

Some suggested uses of music are as follows:

- To create the right atmosphere at the beginning of a seminar, a stage or a theme
- To close a seminar, process, theme or phase
- To enliven breaks with background music
- To encourage relaxation and reduce stress
- To energize and to enliven a tired group
- To create a musical 'anchor', which can be used to recall a previous lesson.

- To create or to change a mood
- To facilitate associative thinking

A list of suggested music is given in Appendix A.

Peripherals

Peripherals are visual material placed around a room to make it attractive and to add to learning. They can consist of colourful pictures, posters, messages which relate to the subject being taught, or affirmations or quotations of a more general nature. They are designed to reinforce the subject being taught in a visual way. Because the messages are perceived at the periphery of conscious awareness they are often absorbed by the subconscious mind in a way which would not be possible if the message were communicated directly. Peripherals can be used to arouse curiosity in advance of the lesson. They can create interest and lead to discussion.

Although most peripherals are in the form of wall displays, it is possible to use other parts of the room. For example, the floor can be used to illustrate the steps or sequence of a procedure and the ceiling could have hanging from it mobiles showing the software keys for a computer package.

Theme messages around the room can set the scene for a whole seminar or series of lessons. For example, the subject could be taught within the setting of an imaginary holiday, a journey or a climbing expedition.

A welcome board can make participants feel welcome from the outset and can do much to enhance their feeling of inclusion in the learning event. On a white board or flip chart simply write the word WELCOME, in colourful letters if possible, and then add the first names of the participants underneath. Or you can draw a cartoon character holding balloons with participants' names in each one. A trainer we know wrote each person's name in glitter for a seminar being held near Christmas. She did this by writing their names in glue and then sprinkling on the glitter. Seeing their names sparkle in this way gave the participants a feeling of pride and pleasure and there were many smiles.

Connecting and engaging

People coming to a training event do so in varying states of readiness for learning. The trainer's job at the outset is to find out what this state is and to create an atmosphere of trust in which open communication can take place and a collaborative learning environment can be built.[2]

The first step is to ask the participants to introduce themselves. People can be quite inhibited about this and it is often best to ask them to work in pairs and for each person to introduce their partner. Some other ideas are given below. The learners can be asked to give certain basic information about themselves, for example their name, their organization, their job and where they live. It is often worthwhile asking them to say more about themselves, for example:

- Their hobbies and/or special interests
- Some special piece of information about themselves
- What they would like to do if they were not in their present job
- What they have done in the past
- Something good that happened to them within the last 24 hours
- Whether there is any particular worry or concern that is occupying their minds at this moment (it is always a good idea to allow participants an opportunity of expressing this, possibly on a daily basis. Just being able to express their concern and to have it acknowledged is often enough to take away its power to interfere with learning)

If the number in the group exceeds around 16, or if time is short, it may be best to get the participants to sit and introduce themselves in table groups.

To confirm what is said and to act as a future resource, it is worth writing a summary of the information provided about each participant on a flip chart. This can be in the form of a colourful mind map, which can form a peripheral for the rest of the course.

Either as part of the interviewing session or shortly afterwards, it is desirable, if not essential, to find out what the participants' aims and expectations from the training event are. This can be done verbally or by getting them to write the aims down. An effective way of doing this is to get them to write their aims on Post-it notes (one aim per note) and to stick them up on a flip chart. The notes can then be arranged easily by themes or subjects and an idea obtained of any common themes.

The introduction session can be enhanced or followed by some physical movement, which can help to break down barriers and make people feel more at ease with each other. The following are some suggestions:

- Participants stand in a circle and throw a koosh ball from one to another, calling out their name and one thing about them which has been mentioned in the introduction.
- Participants move about the room, shake hands with as many others as they can in, say, three minutes, greeting them by name and saying one thing about them.
- Participants move around the room and check with at least three others what three things they have in common about being here today.
- Participants have a questionnaire or 'bingo card' containing items relating to the personal lives of everyone in the group. The task is to

Figure 4.1   *... stand in a circle and ask participants to throw a koosh ball from one to another ...*

find someone who fits the description of each item and so complete the card. For example, find someone who: Likes chocolate; Has been to Australia; Rides a mountain bike; Speaks another language ...

Conclusion

People work best when they feel that they are part of a collaborative working environment. The sooner you get people connected with each other and feeling that they are part of a whole, the sooner they will become open and willing to learn and share with each other.

Notes and references

1 'Viola' is a book and also a set of music CDs written by Hartmut Wagner in German. It is available from the SKILL Institut, Schubertstrasse 3, D-6919 Bammental bei Heidelberg, Germany.
2 Further ideas for introductory activities can be found in the following publications:
Rose, C., Gill, M-J. and Cassone, P. (1991) *Accelerated Learning System 2000: Training and Development Program*, Book 3 (particularly *Activations*, a chapter in this book), available from the publishers, Accelerated Learning Systems Ltd., or the Forge House Centre (see Appendix D—Useful addresses).

Bond, T. (1988) *Games for Social and Life Skills*, Hutchinson, London.
Bourner, T., Martin, V. and Race, P. (1993) *Workshops that Work*, McGraw-Hill, Maidenhead.
Jones, J. and Bearley, W. (1989) *Energizers for Training and Conferences*, Organization Design and Development Inc., King of Prussia, Pennsylvania. Many of the activities can also be used during the other three quadrants of the training cycle.

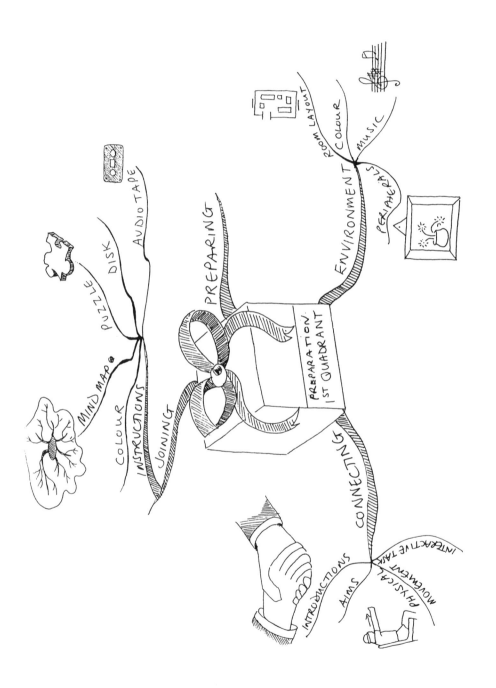

Mind map for Chapter 4—preparation: 1st quadrant

5 Quadrant 2—Presentation

A child explores and learns with no sense of failure or limit. Recovering that child within is the key to accelerated learning

David Meier

Scene *The company training room. A group of 20 tool room operatives were sitting waiting for the lesson to begin. The subject was 'Safety at work'. Few of the men felt that they needed any further instruction in this tedious subject and there was an air of boredom.*

Paul Toogood, the tool room manager, walks into the room. He smiles as he welcomes the operatives and then gives them a brief overview of the programme. He asks them to get into four groups of five and tell each other any stories they know about accidents in toolrooms that they have experienced or heard of. Each group is then invited to tell their best story to the rest of the group.

Paul then announces that he and Tony Wakeman are going to put on a short play. He invites them to make notes and to be prepared at the end to say what thoughts about safety have occurred to them. He then leaves the room, leaving two empty chairs in an open space at the front. Behind the chairs is a big notice saying Stoke Hospital Waiting Room.

Tony Wakeman then appears, heavily bandaged and leaning on a stick. He sits down and starts to read a magazine which has been lying on a low table beside the chair. Paul, also bandaged and on crutches, then comes in and sits beside him. The following dialogue ensues.

Tony: Hello, mate! Been in the wars have you?

Paul: Well, sort of. Got me hand caught up in the pugmill.

Tony: Where's that, then? You at Stokepot?

Paul: Yes, Stokepot. Right shower they are. None of their equipment is guarded. I was lucky not to lose me whole hand.

Tony: Same at my place, Potclays. An overloaded shelf collapsed on me. Broke my leg. Lucky it didn't kill me.

Paul: Yeah. I did have a mate who was killed at work a few months ago. Got his hands wet with the cooling water on a lathe and then handled an electric plug which turned out to be faulty. Electrocuted he was. On the spot.

Tony: Yeah. We had a case like that the other day. One of our lads got all tangled up in the cable of an electric drill he was using. Nearly got strangled when the cable was dragged away by a fork lift truck. No one really bothers about safety much in our lot.

Paul: Same with us. A mate of mine lost the sight of one eye last year. Wasn't wearing goggles while he was doing a grinding job. There weren't enough goggles to go round.

The dialogue proceeds on these lines for a few more minutes. Then Paul and Tony hobble out of the room and return without their bandages. Tony stands by the flip chart, while Paul asks the group to say what points about safety have emerged from the conversation.

The dialogue method of presenting a subject, illustrated briefly above, is one of several ways in which the interest and attention of an audience can be captured and motivation increased. Other methods are described below.

Before making a presentation, however, it is generally sound practice to start with an overview of the lesson, so that right-brained members of the group can develop a global picture of what they are going to learn.

Next, it is often a good idea to invite the participants to work in pairs or small groups and to discover what they already know about the subject. This has several benefits. It makes them actively involved and makes them aware of connections they can make with knowledge they already have. It makes them curious to know more. It breaks down inter-personal barriers and starts to create a cooperative atmosphere. And it tells you as the facilitator what the group already knows and what it does not know. Writing the pooled knowledge on a flip chart in the form of a mind map reinforces visually what has been said and is a reminder throughout the lesson of the knowledge within the group.

Here are some of the ways in which you can make a presentation at the start of a lesson, other than in the conventional way of talking with the aid of an OHP. This of course has its place, but because it is so often used it tends not to awaken interest or to arouse feelings of any sort. For this reason the content is easily forgotten and there is unlikely to be strong motivation to learn more.

When preparing a presentation always bear in mind the needs of the different types of learner. Visual learners will need to see words and/or pictures on flip charts or posters on the walls. Auditory learners will be happy listening to you talking, but they will be stimulated more by several voices and possibly by sound effects. They will like music. Kinesthetic learners will enjoy watching movement and they will be even happier if they can be involved in some kind of movement themselves.

Acting out a dialogue

To prepare a dialogue, start by drawing a mind map of the main teaching points you want to put across. Then think of a situation involving two people in which it is natural for them to talk about the subject. Spend a few minutes relaxing and visualizing the scene, hearing in your mind the conversation they are having. Try to make it realistic and entertaining. Then start to write the dialogue, referring to the mind map and incorporating the teaching points in as natural a way as possible.

The next stage is to find an assistant to act out the part of the other person in the dialogue. This can be a colleague or possibly a member of the group you are teaching. This will only be possible if you know the group and there is an opportunity of having a rehearsal. If possible the dialogue should be memorized, as it is likely to be acted out in a more lively manner than if the actors have to read from a script. The performance does not have to be word perfect. As long as the main points are covered it will be enough to get the group involved and thinking more deeply about the subject. Any points omitted can be added later on the flip chart.

If there is not time for the other person to memorize the lines, you can set up the dialogue in the form of an interview, when it would be natural for them to refer to notes. It adds considerably to the authenticity of the sketch if some props are used. In the lesson described above bandages and a stick were all that were necessary. Very often a hat, a false moustache or an item of unusual clothing are enough. It is very important that there should be a rehearsal. A playlet which goes wrong because of lack of planning can have a counter-productive effect and undermine confidence in the presenters.

It will, of course, not always be possible to find someone who can act as a conversational partner. In this case there are some alternatives. You can create an imaginary person and act as if they were there beside you. There are several examples of this by actors on television. It is worth watching one of these actors and seeing how believable the invisible partner can become.

You can also use glove puppets, which is easier than it might seem. You do not have to be a ventriloquist. All you do is speak in a slightly different manner for each of the puppets and look at the puppet which is talking. If you can add a different accent or dialect this will add interest but it is not essential. The puppet which is speaking should be animated and the other one still. Glove puppets are quite easy to make or they can be bought in various specialist toy shops. A useful source of information is the Puppet Centre, BAC, Lavender Hill, London SW11 5TN.

Finally, you can perform a soliloquy. You could imagine, for example, that you are the manager of a department in a company with an absentee problem. This manager is wearing an unusual hat, a bow tie and perhaps a false nose. He walks up and down and thinks aloud about the problem. Shakespeare often used this device, the most famous example being Hamlet's 'To be or nor to be' soliloquy. Joyce Grenfell, the actress, used it very effectively in solo theatrical performances.

You may feel that you are not an actor and that this style of presentation is not for you. Do not necessarily assume that you have no acting ability. Think for a moment of the different roles you play throughout the day. You might be a parent playing with a small child, a husband or wife reassuring an anxious spouse, a motorist pleading with the traffic police after being stopped for speeding or a manager disciplining an employee for persistent lateness. In each of these cases

Figure 5.1   ... *it will not always be possible to find someone who can act as a conversational partner* ...

your tone of voice and your body language are different. You are playing a role.

If you want to learn more about role playing and acting try taking a course. An excellent one is the weekend Mastery course run by the Actors Institute (see Appendix D for address).

Giving a concert reading

This is an important part of the original language teaching method developed by Dr Lozanov and called Suggestopedia (see Chapter 1). In this method a long dialogue in a foreign language is read by the teacher, accompanied by slow movements (largo or andante) from Baroque music. This type of Baroque music, by composers such as Bach, Vivaldi, Pachelbel and Albinoni has the effect of creating a state of relaxed awareness in the listeners. This state was found by Lozanov to enhance learning considerably and it enabled him to teach languages between two and three times faster than by conventional methods.

He used two types of concert reading. The first was conducted using classical music by composers such as Beethoven and Mozart. This type of music has wide variations in rhythm, volume and pitch and appeals to the emotions. The voice of the teacher harmonizes with the music, and the words become memorable because of their unusual intonation and association with the music. In the second concert the voice of the teacher was normal and the music was Baroque, as described above. In non-language teaching it is unusual for the first concert to be used, so we will describe only the second.

Start by encouraging your participants to do some relaxation and deep breathing exercises. You may wish to give them a copy of the text or dialogue you are going to read to them. This will be helpful to visual learners. The auditory learners will probably prefer to listen with their eyes closed.

Having chosen your music and listened to it beforehand, let it play for a minute or so and then start reading the text, accompanied by the music. Read in short phrases of between 5 and 9 words length and pause between each one so that the listeners can recycle the words in their auditory memory. At the end of the reading, allow the music to play on for a minute or two and then gradually reduce the volume and switch off. If possible introduce a pause before continuing with the next activity.

Concert readings are most effective when they are performed with dialogues. Ideally they should be preceded by acting out the conversation, as described in the preceding paragraph. The concert reading can also be given at the end of a lesson, in the form of a review concert. This is preferred by many trainers to giving it at the beginning. It can be used effectively in conjunction with OHP slides, summarizing the main points of the lesson. When playing music it is important to have a good quality, twin-speaker player, preferably a CD.

Details of music for both types of concert are given in Appendix A.

Telling a story

Everyone likes a story and you will find that your audience will listen attentively. The story could be a case history of a company which has had a problem and has solved it in a creative way. Such stories can be read in business magazines and it might be worth collecting them in a file for future lessons.

Or you can use a metaphor, that is a story quite unconnected with business, but which illustrates a particular point. The *Reader's Digest* is a good source of such stories. Or you can make one up. A book which gives guidance on making up stories which act as metaphors is *Therapeutic Metaphors* (David Gordon, Meta Publications, Cupertino, California).

Making a challenging statement

You might for instance, for a seminar on time management, write on a flip chart a statement such as:

WHAT COUNTS IS NOT THE NUMBER OF HOURS YOU PUT IN BUT HOW MUCH YOU PUT IN THE HOURS

or, for a skills workshop:

WHETHER YOU BELIEVE YOU CAN DO A THING OR NOT, YOU ARE RIGHT
(Henry Ford)

After showing the words on the flip chart (visual) and repeating them (auditory), you might ask the group to work in pairs and discuss the statement (kinesthetic). This would then lead to a group discussion, giving you the opportunity of introducing your topic in a natural way.

Playing an audio or video tape

There are many tapes available commercially which illustrate skills and techniques needed in business. Provided that they are short and relevant, they can make a stimulating start to a lesson. Alternatively you can make off-air recordings of talks, plays or current affairs items. Or you can make your own audio tape, using different voices and sound effects. You can allocate listening roles. For example, some members of the group could be asked to note down all the points they agree with and others the points they disagree with. Others could be asked to look out for ways in which the information might be applied within the company. Another group could be asked to prepare a mind map of the content. All these activities convert passive listening into active participation. Learning takes place at a deeper level.

Involving the group with lists

If, for instance, you wanted to teach eight basic rules for safety in the workplace, you could hand one of the rules to each participant or group of participants. Each of them would then have to try to convince the others that theirs was the most important. The whole group would then have the task of arranging the rules in order of importance.

The group could then be asked to come up with further rules or to modify the existing ones. They might finally produce a list which was more useful and comprehensive than the original one. In this way the participants are actively involved. They think, they talk and they are listened to.

Using visualization

This powerful learning technique is described in Chapter 13. It can be used very effectively at the presentation stage of a lesson. It is particularly effective for right-brained or visual learners, but it may be less so with left-brained or kinesthetic people. Visualization should always start with some relaxation exercises. Playing appropriate music may also enhance its effectiveness considerably.

Visualization can be guided, that is you as the facilitator take charge and provide the listeners with a precise description of what you want them to see in their mind's eye. It can be also semi-guided, which means that you suggest a broad framework and leave them to fill in the details of the picture. Or it can be unguided. In this case you give the listeners a theme or subject and invite them to create their own images.

In all three cases participants should be encouraged to make the images they create as multi-sensory as possible. They should not just see pictures. They should try to hear sounds, experience movement and feelings and even perhaps create sensations of taste or smell. This makes the image more real and thus more memorable. In fact the subconscious mind, which is the seat of memory and the emotions, is often unable to distinguish between a clear multi-sensory image and reality.

To give an example of visualization, the lesson on safety at work could start with a guided imagery session instead of, or in addition to, the role-play described above. Below is an example of how it might sound.

> Take a deep breath and stretch your arms above your head. Slowly lower your arms as you breathe out. Tense and then relax your arms ... your legs ... your stomach ... and your face muscles. Feel the weight of your arms and then of your legs. Enjoy the pleasant feeling of relaxation which you may now begin to experience throughout your body. Allow your attention to become fixed on your breath ... If your thoughts wander, bring them gently back to the breath ...
>
> As you are sitting there, feeling comfortable and relaxed, allow an image to form in your mind of the toolroom where you work. Imagine you are there

now. See what is going on around you. Hear the sounds. Feel the movement of your body and hands as you work at your machine.

Now look at one of the lathes. A young apprentice is working there. He has long hair. As he bends forward the hair is falling dangerously close to the rotating chuck ... Suddenly there is a scream. His hair has become entangled in the machinery. He is being dragged towards it. You rush over and press the emergency isolation switch. He is within an inch of being scalped. As you release him and escort him to the first aid centre, your thoughts are focused on what steps could be taken to prevent this kind of accident happening again ...

Now you see an older man with his hands dripping from the cooling water of his grinding machine. He is stretching out his hand towards an electric switch which you know is faulty ...

You can go on in this way to create all the situations that you want the participants to consider concerning safety at their place of work. Bear in mind, when giving guided visualizations on this kind of subject, that you may be stirring memories of past traumas and that some people might experience negative reactions. Try if possible to conclude each visualization with a positive outcome, as in the case above.

To give a semi-guided visualization, you start with the same relaxation exercise and then invite the participants to move in their imagination from one piece of machinery to another. You might suggest that they look at the equipment, see it in operation and imagine all the things that could possibly happen to cause a danger to the person operating it.

For an unguided visualization, you might invite the participants to imagine themselves in any toolroom of their choice, perhaps an imaginary one, and to walk around it, considering everything in it which might have a bearing on safety.

There is no limit to the ways in which you can use visualization to introduce a subject. Here are a few more examples:

- Seeing how an electronic circuit works from the inside, perhaps from the point of view of one of the electrons
- Seeing yourself performing a new job successfully
- Seeing yourself in a situation in the past in which your performance was not as you might have wished. Then going through it again, this time performing as you would have wished
- Seeing the ideal solution to a problem
- Seeing excellent relationships within a department

When the visualization is finished, always bring the participants gently back to a fully conscious state. You might do this in something like the following way:

Now bring your awareness back to the present time and the room you are in. Be aware of the chair and of your body sitting on the chair. Be aware of the people around you. I am going to count from one to five. On the count of five you will open your eyes, stretch and look around you. You will feel fully awake and alert, ready to take an active part in the lesson ... One ... two ... three ... four ... FIVE. Eyes open. Stretch. Take a deep breath. Look around the room, at the walls, the ceiling, the floor. You are now fully awake and alert.

At this stage it is often useful to allow a short time for the participants to reflect on their experience and perhaps to write down some of their thoughts. They might also be given the opportunity of sharing their experience with a partner and possibly with the whole group. This can often lead to a stimulating discussion which can become an ideal introduction to the teaching points.

The methods of introducing a lesson described above are not exhaustive. With some thought and imagination you will be able to invent others. Often a conventional approach, using an OHP and/or flip chart, will be both adequate and preferable. But the more unusual and entertaining you can make the introduction to the lesson the more interest you will arouse and the more likely it will be that learning will take place.

Further ideas for visualization are given in Chapter 13.

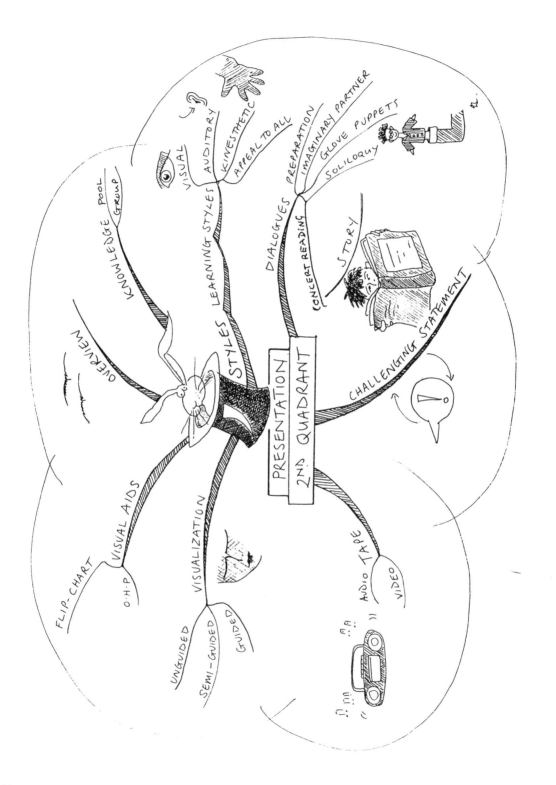

Mind map for Chapter 5—presentation: 2nd quadrant

6 Quadrant 3—Practice

The aim of education is to convert the mind into a living fountain, not a reservoir

John Mason

Scene *The company training room. David Brookes, the kiln manager, had been working with Tony Wakeman and was beginning to adopt some of his training techniques. He was now giving the second lesson on biscuit firing to a group of trainees. The first lesson, given with Tony's help, went well. He started with a dialogue, followed by some group work and used a mind map and some physical activities to reinforce memory. He was now about to start the first activation of the lesson.*

'Right,' said David. 'I want you all to stand and line up in the order of the date you joined Glospot.'

There was a lot of talk and laughter as the 15 trainees sorted themselves out into the required order. David then asked them to pair off and sit down with their new partner. He gave each pair two sets of flash cards containing questions about the lesson. Each person had to spend five minutes putting the questions on the flash cards to their partner and drilling them until they got the answers right.

'Okay,' called out David, when the 10 minutes were up. 'I'd like you all to stand up and form a circle.' The pairs seemed reluctant to break off from their 'drilling'. They were clearly enjoying it, but in a minute or two everyone was standing expectantly in a circle.

'Right,' said David, smiling and looking round at everyone. 'I'd like you to imagine that you are all part of a giant brain. Each one of you is a neuron—a nerve cell—in the brain. Every neuron contains some information and all the neurons together contain all the information about biscuit firing. I'm going to throw the koosh ball at one of you neurons. When you catch it, you have 15 seconds to confer with the neurons on your right and left before giving me the answer. This is how neurons work. They confer with each other to come up with an answer to a problem.'

David looked slowly around the circle. 'What is the advantage of having a percentage of cristobalite in a clay body?' he asked and threw the red koosh ball at Jim, a young trainee who had only joined the company three weeks before. He answered confidently. 'It gives extra shrinking and reduces crazing.'

'Well done, that neuron!' exclaimed David. 'That's exactly right.' The game proceeded until everyone had had a chance to answer a question. There was a feeling of energy and excitement in the group and some disappointment expressed when the game came to an end.

'Now for a team game,' announced David. He got them to divide into two groups, which he named the Cristobalites and the Copper Oxiders. 'I'm going to call out 10 statements about firing. Some of them will be true and others will be false. If they are true you must raise your arms. If they're false you must sit down on the floor. The first team to have all the members acting together correctly wins a point for that question. The team which gets most points wins the competition.'

This is how a lesson introducing the activation stage of a lesson might start. This is the third of the four quadrants of the creative trainer learning cycle. The activities are directed by the facilitator, but many of them require groups to work semi-autonomously. It is more of a cooperative approach to learning. It is at this stage that the dynamic of the group becomes particularly important, for if this is not supportive and cooperative little learning will take place.

Group dynamic

It is useful when considering group dynamic to bear in mind the distinction between 'task-oriented' and 'process-oriented' activities. Most training in industry is task-oriented, that is, it has a specific job-related aim, as in this case. Increasingly, however, there is a recognition of the value of process-oriented work, that is, to use interactions within the group as an opportunity to improve communication skills, creative thinking, team cooperation and stress reduction.

The two are not mutually exclusive. On the contrary, they can be combined to enhance the effectiveness of training, producing accelerated learning and heightened motivation. This combination is an important aspect of being a creative trainer. Every task-oriented session should be combined with some process work in order to produce deeper learning and the development of individual potential.

Most groups pass through stages in the development of their dynamic, and different activities are appropriate at each one.[1] The first stage is that of defensiveness. Trust is low and anxiety is high. People are not willing to take risks. You need to build up trust through a series of non-threatening activities. These include working in pairs and small groups, changing seating and encouraging people to get to know each other. Unfamiliar activities should be carefully explained beforehand, with their purpose clearly spelt out.

Next comes the stage of working through defensiveness. Trust should be building and anxiety reducing. Now you can be more adventurous and you can encourage people to take risks. Physical energy-raising and relaxing exercises can be introduced. You can introduce guided visualization with articulation to partners, role play with dressing up and other unfamiliar activities. Sharing of feelings and attitudes can begin to take place.

The next stage may or may not happen, but you must be ready for it. It is sometimes known as 'storming'. Personality differences have emerged and may result in clashes, either between participants or between one or more participants and yourself. Some participants may feel that their expectations are not being met. Others may be feeling aggressive, or aggrieved with the organization, and take it out on you. It is important not to be upset by such behaviour, which can be quite threatening. Listen and let people express their feelings. This may be enough to defuse the situation. Or there may be concrete action which you can take to overcome the problem, such as taking a complaint up with management.

The group should now move naturally into the fourth stage, that of 'authentic behaviour'. Trust is high and anxiety is low. There is openness, risk-taking and sharing. At this stage the group can to some extent take care of the learning process. Sub-groups can prepare and deliver mini-lessons of their own, organize group activities and make connections with their actual work.

The final stage is that of 'closure'. It is time for the group to look back and assess how much they have learned and what they have got out of working together. It is time to acknowledge the contribution which the members have made and to evaluate the effectiveness of the trainer's work. This can be done either verbally, using a flip chart with two columns—'What went well?' and 'What could have gone better?'—or by handing out opinion forms. If the group has bonded well, there may be scope for arranging further informal meetings.

The following is a selection of activities which fall generally under the heading of Primary Activation in the four-quadrant learning cycle. They involve a certain amount of control by the trainer, but some of the initiative is beginning to pass to the participants. This corresponds to Heron's cooperative stage. They are divided into three types—individual, partnered and group activities.

Individual activities

(IA.1) Mind mapping

Ask individuals to mind map a presentation, an article, an audio tape, an experience, a hope or expectation, a previous lesson or anything relative to their learning that might be significant.[2]

(IA.2) Learner's choice

Provide a smorgasbord of materials and let learners choose the learning method that fits them best. For example, in the lesson on biscuit firing there might be an audio cassette, a written handout or an opportunity for hands-on experimenting with a kiln.

Figure 6.1   *... provide a period in which learners can be alone or away from the group to reflect ...*

(*IA.3*) Quiet time

Provide a period in which learners can be alone or away from the group to reflect, to re-energize, to formulate questions, or simply to organize their thoughts about what they are learning.

✳ (*IA.4*) Question board

Give learners Post-it notes. Ask them to write all the questions about a subject on the notes—one question per note. Post them on a board or flip chart. When all the notes are posted, ask the learners to return to the board and pick off as many of the other people's notes as they think they can answer. Then go round the room and ask everyone to answer the questions they have selected. The questions remaining on the board (there may not be any) can be answered by the facilitator.

(*IA.5*) Lesson evaluation

Ask each learner to write a five-minute evaluation of a lesson on a large index card in colour, indicating what worked best for them and what enhancements might make the lesson better.

Partnered activities

(*PA.1*) Articulation

Ask partners to describe to each other their reactions to what has just been presented.

(*PA.2*) Five questions

Ask each partner to ask the other five questions about what has just been presented.

(*PA.3*) Board game

Give each pair the same pack of cards with questions written on them and a board game (photocopied on a piece of paper). For playing pieces they can use coins or small objects. A correctly answered question advances a person's playing piece.

(*PA.4*) Flashcards

Distribute flashcards (of acronyms, terms, components, processes, etc.) to each partnership. Have partner A drill partner B for a short time, say five minutes. Then, at a signal from the facilitator reverse roles.

(*PA.5*) Materials creation

Ask partnerships to make a colourful mind map or graphic or job aid about what they have just learned. Give them only a short time to do this.

(*PA.6*) Peripheral creation

Ask partnerships to make a peripheral for the room about what they have just learned: an object, a wall decoration, a mobile, a floor decoration, a table-top display, etc.

Team-based activities

(*TBA.1*) Activations for introductions and breaks

(*TBA.1a*) 'How do you feel now?'

Divide the group into pairs and ask each pair to describe to the other how they feel now at the beginning of the course. After this has been articulated, tell the group that they will be asked to write their feelings on two flip charts. One chart should be placed at one end of the room and the other near the exit. On the flip chart near the exit, write the question 'How do you want to feel on leaving the course?' On the other flip chart, write 'How do you feel right now?' Each participant then gets up from their chair and writes a word describing their feelings on both charts. If there is time you can review and connect with the group. In this way the participants share their feelings and realize which ones they have in common.

(*TBA.1b*) Name game

The trainer asks each learner to choose a descriptive adjective that starts with the same letter as the learner's first name—one that they believe also describes them appropriately in some way. The class forms a circle and, as each person introduces themself, they repeat all the names that have been announced before them.[3]

(*TBA.1c*) Clairvoyant

At the beginning of the course divide the participants into pairs and ask each person to tell their partner what they know about them, even though they may be strangers. Give them the following instructions:

> You are to imagine that you have psychic powers and in the exercise of these powers you can make intuitive guesses about your partner. Your task is to make statements about the other person, using the following sentences as a guide: I see that you ... I think that you ... I imagine that you ... You sound ...

> Your partner (the listener) will take notes for five minutes on what you have said and then you will reverse roles.

Depending on the size of the group, people can report back what was said about them and make corrections if necessary.

(*TBA.1d*) Hot ball

The trainer tosses a 'hot ball' (koosh ball or foam rubber ball) to the learners, asking them questions about the content of the lesson. Learners may 'pass' on a particular turn, but should be returned to later by the trainer. The learners can also toss the ball to each other and initiate the questions.

(TBA.1e) Crossword

Divide the group into threes or fours and give each group a large sheet of paper with a blank crossword marked on it. Give them a list of clues relevant to the learning and a set of letters that are answers to the clues. The team can then use the letters to create the crossword, using Post-it stickers or cards, or simply writing in pencil so that they may be erased if necessary.

(TBA.1f) The windmill

Everyone stands and the trainer reviews the important points so far covered. As each point is called out, the learners hold their left hand in front of them while making a huge circle with their right arm, repeating out loud the lesson point and bringing their hands together in a clap as they say it.

(TBA.2) Group brain

Here the facilitator assumes the role of client and the class as a whole becomes the brain of the company employee. The facilitator makes a statement and throws the ball into the brain. A 'neuron' catches it, and, since no neuron works alone, has 15 seconds or so to confer with the neuron on the right and on the left to formulate a response. The neuron gives the response and throws the ball back to the facilitator for another exchange. The action can be stopped at any time to ask other parts of the brain if they agree with the response just made or if they could improve upon it or offer an alternate response.

(TBA.3) Map what you know

The group constructs a group mind map of the contents of the lesson just presented. Alternatively they can be asked to do it before the lesson, in order to find out how much they already know about the subject. This will make apparent any gaps in the knowledge of the group and allow the facilitator to fill them in.

(TBA.4) Terminology bingo

The trainer chooses 25^+ technical terms, symbols or abbreviations that the learners have previously encountered and prepares a small bingo card for each one. She puts 12 of the cards on a bingo board, leaving other spaces blank. The remaining items are put on the margins of the board.

The learners then complete their own bingo boards by choosing items from the list of available choices on the margin. Next, the trainer begins to read definitions of each of the 25^+ terms. Learners put an 'x' over the term on their board that corresponds to the definition given. The winner is the first learner to cross out five terms in a row, and who can also correctly define each of the terms in that row.

(TBA.5) Definition match

Make up two identical sets of cards. One set contains a technical term or abbreviation and the other a description of that term or abbreviation. Give out the cards equally and ask the trainees to find a person who has the matching card.

(TBA.6) Television game show

There are many television games which can be adapted to enliven a question and answer session, for example:

1 Use a roulette wheel to pick questions that have been divided into two piles—red or black, corresponding, perhaps, to hard and easy.
2 Divide questions up into £10, £20 and £50 questions. The teams compete for the most money. Alternatively, the questions can be stuck on a board, covered by an appropriate £ value.
3 Use a race game board from a proprietary game. Each correct answer moves the team forward one or more spaces.

(TBA.7) Stand or fall

The learners divide into two teams and form circles for easy communication. The trainer reads a series of true/false questions that have been prepared in advance. The teams must discuss and agree on an answer and then answer in unison, either all raising their hands (true) or crossing their arms (false). For more physical involvement they can sit on the floor instead of crossing their arms. The first team to respond correctly to the question wins the point. The team with the most points is the winner.

(TBA.8) Paint a picture of success

In teams ask participants to describe or draw or act out the picture of a successful learner who is a master of the skills about to be taught. Ask the teams to represent a detailed picture of how the learner would sound, feel and act.

(TBA.9) Memory mime

The trainer prepares flashcards containing terms which have been taught and the learners are given one or more cards. They sit in a circle and take it in turns to go to the front of the room and mime the term on the flashcard. The class guess the term. They are then shown the card, say the term aloud and mime it together. If it is important that the terms are learnt in sequence, the class can repeat each of the previous terms from memory before saying the new one.

(TBA.10) Sequence shuffle

The trainer prepares flashcards, each one describing a different part of a system, department or stage in a production line. One card is given to each learner and the learner with the card which represents the beginning of the sequence goes to the front of the room and describes to the rest of the group the significance of the card they are holding. The learner holding the next card in the sequence goes to the front of the room, stands next to the first person, describes the card they are holding and the relationship to the previous card. This continues until all the cards are used. The last learner will be describing their card and the entire sequence of the system.

(TBA.11) Group sculpture

Have prepared a set of questions appropriate to the learning that is to follow. One such question could be: 'How much do you know about this topic?' One end of the room will represent that they know a lot and the other end that they know little. People will then position themselves along this continuum. You may then ask people who know to share their knowledge with others.

Notes and references

1 These stages are described in greater detail in Heron, J. (1989) *The Facilitator's Handbook* (pp. 26–27), Kogan Page, London.
2 Exercises 1A.1 to TBA.1a and exercise TBA.2 are taken, with kind permission, from David Meier's Accelerated Learning workshops. David Meier can be contacted at The Center for Accelerated Learning, 1103 Wisconsin Street, Lake Geneva, WI 53147, USA.
3 Exercises TBA.1 to TBA.10 (excluding exercise TBA.2) are taken, with kind permission, from Rose, C., Gill, M-J. and Cassone, P. (1991) *Accelerated Learning System 2000: Training and Development Program*, Accelerated Learning Systems Ltd., Aylesbury. This is available from the publisher (see Appendix D for address).

Unattributed exercises are contributed by the authors.

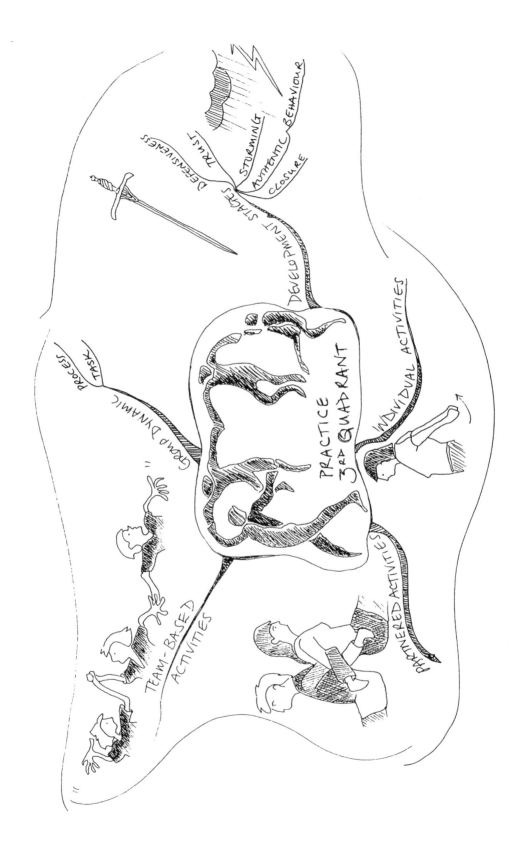

Mind map for Chapter 6—practice: 3rd quadrant

7 Quadrant 4—Performance

*The turtle only makes progress
when his neck is stuck out*

Rollo May

Scene *Jill Bird felt slightly apprehensive as she awaited the arrival of the group of directors and managers. As managing director she was making herself vulnerable by conducting a training session at all, let alone one run on the 'creative training' lines proposed by Tony Wakeman. However, the first session, when she had introduced the subject of 'Society and Environment',[1] had gone well, as had the primary activation session the following week. She was now about to facilitate a secondary activation, a week later, and she was not sure how it would go. Mary Weller, the finance director, had been sceptical about the whole idea of social responsibility and there had been a clash of opinion between her sons, Jack, the production director, and Warren, the marketing director.*

This so-called 'fourth quadrant' of Tony's meant that she would have to surrender a lot of control and she wondered whether she could trust the group not to make a mess of it. The door opened and the group entered together, having just come from having coffee in the outer office. They were chatting and laughing—a good sign, thought Jill. The group dynamic seems to be okay. She had put on some lively music and she noticed that several people's step quickened in time with the music. She asked them to stand in a circle.

'Good morning everyone,' she said, looking round at each person in turn and smiling. 'Let's have a short checking-in session. On a scale of one to ten, how does your energy feel this morning? You might like to add one word, too, to describe how you're feeling. I'll throw the koosh ball at the first person and then you can throw it to anyone you choose.'

The ball went round the group and a range of energy states were reported, accompanied by phrases such as 'bright and breezy', 'down in the dumps', 'raring to go'.

Jill then initiated another game with the koosh ball. On receipt of the ball, each participant had to state one of the responsibilities of the professional manager with regard to society and the environment. Wendy Brown, the office supervisor, was the first person to receive the ball.

'The actions we plan to take—what sort of effects they may have on people outside the business,' said Wendy, just managing to catch the ball and throwing it awkwardly to Jack Bird.

'Keep up to date on proposed legislation and be prepared to comment on it,' said Jack, in a somewhat bored voice, as he threw the ball with an underhand flick of the wrist to Syd Mosdell, the purchasing manager, who was not expecting it and dropped it.

'Er . . . communicate to the public truthfully and without intent to mislead. I think that was it.' Syd looked questioningly at Jill, who nodded in confirmation. He threw the ball carefully to Warren Bird, who caught it in the style of a cricketer and paused for a moment, thinking.

'Conserve resources . . . especially when they're non-renewable?' said Warren tentatively. The group nodded approvingly and he threw the ball high in the air to Margaret Crawford, the design manager.

There was a silence, while Margaret furrowed her brow in thought. 'I'm sorry, I'll have to pass,' she said, and threw the ball on to Roger Martin, the moulding shop manager.

'Pollution,' responded Roger promptly. 'Seek to avoid destruction of resources by pollution. Oh, and have a contingency plan to deal with a disaster.'

'Very good indeed,' said Jill Bird, with a broad smile. 'I see you've all done your homework. This morning we're going to look at these five areas of responsibility in greater depth—and you are going to do the work!'

The group exchanged glances. There were a number of wry smiles.

'Okay. I'd like you to get into groups of three. I'm going to give each group a card with one of the "society and environment" responsibilities on it. I want the group to discuss and agree on what is the most frequent obstacle to putting this precept into practice. You will have five minutes for this.'

As soon as the groups had formed and were sitting together, Jill gave out their cards and there was a buzz of animated conversation. After five minutes Jill rang a small hand bell and called for attention.

'Right, next I want you to take one of these blank cards and write on it a short description of the obstacle you have chosen.'

Jill gave each of the groups a 12.5cm × 7.5cm card and paused while they wrote on it. 'Now I want you to give your card to the group on your right.' The cards were handed round in a clockwise direction and studied by their new owners.

'Okay,' said Jill. 'You have 10 minutes to think of a solution to the problem on the card. At the end of that time I'm going to call on each group to present a solution to the problem.'

As the groups worked on the problems they had been presented with, Jill walked from one to another and listened to their discussions. She was pleased with some of the imaginative ideas which were being expressed. When the 10 minutes were up she rang her bell again and asked each group in turn to give a five-minute presentation of their problem and proposed solution. She was particularly impressed by the group discussing the conservation of resources. They came up with an interesting proposal for recycling the clay from rejected mouldings.

After that she gave them a guided visualization of the effect on the local rivers of toxic materials such as sodium oxide, barium and boron, all of which were at times pumped out of the factory as waste. They then had to write an imaginative piece from the point of view of one of the creatures which used the river—fish, birds, otters, etc. They read this to a partner and then shared their experience with the group.

Finally, she asked them to work in groups of three and four to produce an imaginary television documentary designed to raise awareness among local companies of the need for increased responsibility toward the local community and the environment. This took most of the afternoon and the group volunteered to work late so that all the sub-groups could make presentations of their 'story boards'.

At the end of the day everyone in the group seemed convinced of the need for positive action to make the company more accountable for the effect it was having on its environment. Several people commented to Jill how much they had enjoyed the day.

Jill retired to her office and poured herself a stiff whiskey. 'So it worked,' she thought to herself. 'Jack and Warren got on well together. Wendy seemed quite enthusiastic. And they all seem to have really taken the idea on board. So it's really okay to hand over responsibility and to encourage people to enjoy themselves. But I can't see them ever going back to the old format of OHP and talk. And I don't think I'd want to.'

The fourth quadrant lesson described above corresponds to Heron's autonomous stage. Although in this case the trainer sets up the activities, the way they are carried out is largely up to the participants. As the group enters the 'authentic behaviour' stage (see Chapter 6) it could be given responsibility for designing exercises itself.

The subject covered in this lesson of Jill Bird's is an important one—the responsibility of a company to its outside environment. The five points revised in the koosh ball game are in fact the ones made in the Institute of Management's Code of Conduct.[2] A code of ethics is essential if morale in a company is to be maintained and its long-term future assured. People will only feel a sense of loyalty and commitment to an organization if its values are such as to inspire them.

The question of ethics in a wider perspective is explored in a number of books. Three recommended ones are: *Good Business* (Carmichael and Drummond), *The Power of Ethical Management* (Peale and Blanchard) and *The Greening of Business* (Davis).[3] These books could form the basis of training sessions similar to the one described in some detail above.

The activities described below are listed under three headings—individual, partnered and team-based.

Individual activities

(*IA.6*) Material creation

Ask individuals to create a gift or gifts for subsequent classes in the form of a peripheral, a job aid, a mnemonic device, an icon pamphlet or cartoon book, a poem, a testimonial or some instrument of encouragement, a game, a song or anything else which they can think of.[4]

(*IA.7*) Mental imagery

Ask learners to rehearse a piece of knowledge or a skill in their minds. Provide them with a cassette recorder onto which they can record their thoughts and play them back. The process of articulation will itself stimulate their memory and imagination. Playing the tape back will be a reminder and a stimulus to further thinking about the subject.

(*IA.8*) Preparing to teach

Ask learners to create something they can share with someone else during a partnered or group activity. Or tell them that they will have to teach what they are learning to someone else in the room at a certain point in the day.

(*IA.9*) Research project

Assign each learner an individual research project. Ask them to research the answer either inside or outside the classroom as appropriate and report back to the class.

Partnered activities

(*PA.7*) Help your partner

Ask partners to spend time helping each other prepare for a mastery demonstration or knowledge assessment or skill performance (euphemisms for test!), that will be administered in a specified amount of time.

(*PA.8*) Activity creation

Ask partners to prepare a skit or role play or action learning exercise, or game or review exercise for the class.

(PA.9) Ad design

Ask partners to take five or 10 minutes to design a magazine or newspaper advertisement for a product they are learning about, stressing its main feature and benefits.

(PA.10) Teaching project

Subcontract a part of the curriculum to a partnership. Ask them to read up on this part and make a presentation to the class about it that will be fun, colourful, active and (above all) effective in helping people learn and remember.

Team-based activities

(TBA.12) Twenty questions

Give each team a specified time (not too long) to come up with 20 questions from the learning material. The teams ask each other questions, one at a time and back and forth, allowing a specified time (15–30 seconds) for an answer to be given. Correct answers earn a point.

(TBA.13) Review project

Assign teams the task of providing a review for an aspect of the learning material. Their review can be a game, an exercise, a concert review or anything they feel will contribute to the learning and long-term integration of the material.

(TBA.14) Materials creation

Assign teams the job of making learning materials that could be used in subsequent classes to help others learn. Such materials could include job aids, peripherals, mind maps, learning games, action learning scenarios, video vignettes, cartoon books, objects, presentation graphics, metaphors, mnemonics, songs, limericks, etc.

(TBA.15) Group consulting

Announce towards the end of a course that participants are going to help their colleagues solve a work-based problem. Each person comes up with a problem for the group and the group seeks understanding of the situation. The group then brainstorms ideas to solve the problem and the problem holder listens. Someone is appointed to take notes or create a mind map of the answers.

(TBA.16) Super salesperson

The trainer prepares one 'super salesperson' badge per three or four trainees and distributes them to groups of this number. Each group brainstorms an idea that enhances the core lesson or a solution to a problem. The group agrees on a representative, their super salesperson, who will wear the badge. The group then agrees on how to 'sell' the idea or solution to the remainder of the class. The salesperson has to visit the other groups to try to sell their idea. The 'buyers' simply listen and make notes. After all the groups have been visited they decide which idea they will buy. The idea with the most offers wins.[5]

(TBA.17) Playlets

After giving the group an input on a particular piece of theory or concept, divide the group into three or four sub-groups and ask each to devise a playlet. They are to use themselves as props to act out the process or concept.

(TBA.18) Press releases

The learners divide into teams and are asked to create a press release for a company newsletter. This will describe the benefits of the product/programme that is the subject of the training session. The teams read their press releases to the class. The texts are displayed on the wall.

(TBA.19) Be a television documentary director

Ask mini-groups of three or four to imagine that they are a team of television directors. Their job is to create a really exciting documentary of the day's training session, that will make what has been learned memorable to another audience. There are no budgetary restrictions. The teams present their 'storyboard' to the class, which decides on 'Academy Awards'.

(TBA.20) Fantasy land

The learners divide into teams and prepare a fairy tale or metaphorical story. To write the story the teams choose a world (sport, film, space or well-known fairy tale setting) and create a story that uses the points of the lesson. Each team then reads or performs their story to the class and an applause vote is held for the favourite story.

Notes and references

1   From Evers, S. (1993) 'The Manager as a Professional' (pp. 55–57), Institute of Management, Corby. This document supports and expands upon the Code of Conduct and Guides to Professional Management Practice of the Institute of Management and is available from the Institute at Management House, Cottingham Road, Corby, Northants NN17 1TT.

2   Ibid.

3   Carmichael, S. and Drummond, J. (1989) *Good Business*, Business Books Ltd., London.
    Peale, N.V. and Blanchard, K. (1988) *The Power of Ethical Management*, Heinemann Kingswood, London.
    Davis, J. (1991) *Greening Business*, Basil Blackwell, Oxford.

4   Exercises 1A.6 to TBA.14 are taken, with kind permission, from David Meier's Accelerated Learning workshops. See Chapter 6, note 2, for address.

5 Exercises TBA.16 and TBA.18–20 are taken, with kind permission, from
   Rose, C., Gill, M-J. and Cassone, P. (1991) *Accelerated Learning System 2000:
   Training and Development Program*, Accelerated Learning Systems Ltd.,
   Aylesbury. See Appendix D for address.

Unattributed exercises are provided by the authors.

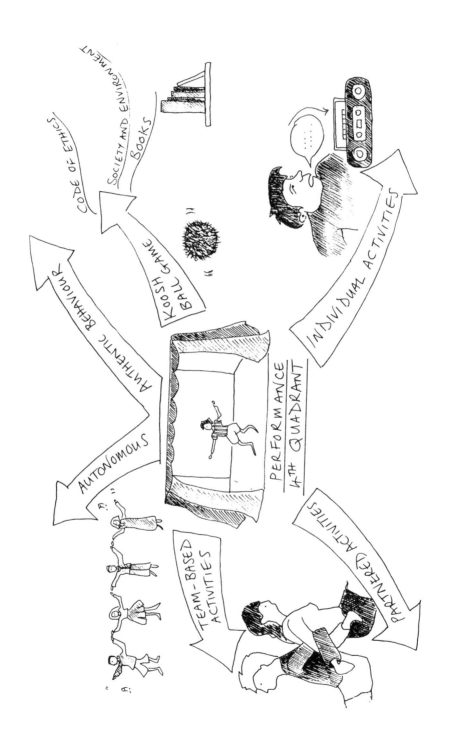

Mind map for Chapter 7—performance: 4th quadrant

PART 3

The building blocks

8 Thinking and learning styles

*Your reason and your passion are
the rudder and the sails of your
seafaring soul.
If either your sails or your rudder be
broken, you can but toss and drift,
or else be held at a standstill in mid
seas.
For reason, ruling alone, is a force
confining; and passion, unattended,
is a flame that burns to its own
destruction.*

from *The Prophet*, Kahlil Gibran

Scene *The boardroom of Glospot Ltd. Tony Wakeman was conducting
a workshop for a small group of managers on thinking and learning
styles.*

'I'd like you to imagine,' said Tony, smiling and giving eye contact to the
eight people sitting around him in a half circle, 'that it is Christmas. You are
approached by your young nephew, who has been given a working model of a
bulldozer. It is in kit form and he does not know how to go about assembling
it. You agree to help him. Do you read the instructions or do you immediately
have a go at assembling it?'

There was a short silence, followed by a variety of opinions. Jack Bird, Roger
Martin, David Brooks, Graham Casson and Wendy Brown said they would
read the instructions. Warren Bird, Margaret Crawford and Mick O'Tool
said they would have a go.

'So what does this tell you about the way you think?' asked Tony.

'That we're all different?' hazarded Graham.

'Indeed,' replied Tony. 'For instance, some of us like to tackle problems in a
step-by-step, logical way. They are the ones who read the instructions before
tackling a task. Others like to try to see a pattern, get an overview and maybe

use their intuition. They have a go at assembling the kit. The first group are usually what is known as left-brained and the second right-brained.'

'What difference does it make?' asked Jack Bird abruptly. 'I thought we were here to find out how to learn better. I'd like some practical techniques.'

'There you go again,' said Warren Bird, casting his eyes up to the ceiling.

'Actually it makes quite a lot of difference,' replied Tony evenly. 'You see we all have different thinking styles, and unless we know what our own style is, we're not going to make the best use of our brains.'

'Don't we all use different senses to learn?' asked Warren. 'I've read somewhere that some people like to see new information and others to hear it.'

'That's very true,' replied Tony. 'I was coming to that. And a third group of people like to get involved physically. They're called kinesthetic learners. The other two are called visual and auditory learners. There's another thing too. We don't just have one kind of intelligence. We all have at least seven.'

'Not all. There are some people who don't have any,' remarked Jack Bird, glancing at his brother and looking studiously out of the window.

Although the brain has tremendous potential for storing information and reorganizing it in creative ways, we rarely use its full potential. As mentioned in the Preface, some psychologists think that we use less than one per cent.

This is an important concept for you as a trainer. The key to unlocking the potential of each person's unused brain capacity is recognition of their brain dominance. The fundamental distinction is whether the dominance is toward the right or the left hemisphere. But there is a further distinction between whether the brain is dominantly cerebral or limbic. The cerebral part of the brain is concerned with thought; the limbic part with emotions.

As a trainer you need to know how your own brain functions so that you can make allowances for it and not permit any one tendency to unbalance your presentations. You need to know which are the under-developed parts of your brain, so that you can take steps to activate them. You need also to be aware of your trainees' brain dominance so that you can present information to them in an appropriate way and help them overcome possible learning blocks.

There are a number of questionnaires designed to assess the way an individual's brain works. Four of the best known are the Herrmann Brain Dominance Instrument (HBDI),[1] the Hemisphere Centre Profile (HCP),[2] the Brain Map[3] and the Gregorc Thinking Style Test.[4]

Herrmann Brain dominance instrument whole brain model

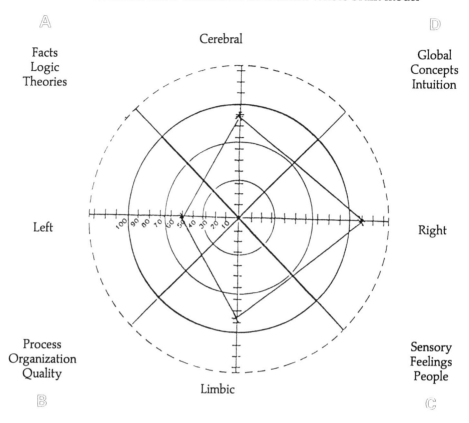

Figure 8.1 *A typical workshop profile* © *1986, Ned Herrmann*

Herrmann Brain Dominance Instrument

The HBDI (see Figure 8.1), which is perhaps the most complete and instructive, defines four types of thinker/learner, as follows.

Upper left quadrant A

This type of person learns best by:

- Acquiring and quantifying facts
- Applying analysis and logic
- Thinking through ideas
- Building cases
- Forming theories

They respond best to:

- Formalized lectures
- Data-based content
- Financial/technical case discussions
- Text books and bibliographies

This group of learners like setting goals and making plans. They work well alone. They like to see the application of theories, to work to timetables and to make notes and classify them. On the negative side, they can be impatient with other people's viewpoints, become preoccupied with detail and lack imagination.

Lower left quadrant B

This type of person learns best by:

- Organizing, structuring and sequencing content
- Evaluating and testing theories
- Acquiring skills through practice
- Implementing course content

They respond to:

- Good planning
- Sequential ordering
- Case discussions
- Text books
- Lectures
- Structure

This group like to understand everything, are curious and enjoy problems and working things out well on paper. They like to set clear goals and are precise and thorough.

On the other hand, they often want too much information before getting down to a task, are reluctant to try new approaches and they tend to get bogged down in theory. They like to do things in a set way and do not trust their feelings.

Lower right quadrant C

This type of person learns best by:

- Listening and sharing ideas
- Integrating experiences within themselves
- Moving and feeling
- Harmonizing with the content
- Emotional involvement

They respond to:

- Experiential opportunities
- Music
- People-oriented case discussions
- Group interaction

These learners become totally involved in something which interests them, they work well with other people and are willing to try out new ideas.

Weaknesses are that they need to be interested in a subject to work at it, they do not like planning, are not good at organizing time and are not concerned with detail.

Upper right quadrant D

This type of person learns by:

- Taking the initiative
- Exploring hidden possibilities
- Using intuition
- Self-discovery
- Constructing concepts
- Synthesizing content

They respond to:

- Spontaneity and free flow
- Experiential opportunities
- Playfulness
- Future-oriented case discussions
- Visual displays
- Individuality
- Being involved
- Aesthetic considerations

These learners often see new ways of doing things and come up with creative solutions. They like to see long-term implications and the whole picture. They listen well, share ideas and see connections between subjects.

On the other hand, they are bored by detail, do not organize work well, work in bursts of energy, are easily distracted and often forgetful.

The Herrmann Brain Dominance Instrument produces a profile of an individual's thinking style. Figure 8.1 shows a profile of someone who is dominant in the right brain limbic quadrant C, with strong secondary dominances in the B and D quadrants. This means that they have the ability to switch back and forth between the B, C and D thinking styles. They are weak in the A quadrant.

To gain an individual HBDI profile it is necessary to obtain and fill in a somewhat lengthy questionnaire and to have it marked and analysed by the Ned Herrmann Institute. Their address is shown in Appendix D. Questionnaires can also be obtained from Forge House Centre for Language and Life Skills.

Another aspect of the way the brain processes information is its preference for input through some of the senses rather than others. Some people need to see new information before they can process and retain it. They are visual learners and they respond well to visual aids such as OHP transparencies, slides and flip charts. Others prefer to listen to the spoken word. These are auditory learners and they are quite happy listening to lectures. A third group likes to be involved physically with any new learning. They are the so-called kinesthetic learners. They like hands-on experience, group discussions and role play.

A questionnaire entitled 'How clear is your mind's eye?', designed to give an indication of an individual's preferred sensory mode and ability to create multi-sensory mental images, is also included in Appendix B.

Obviously it will not be possible to carry out the sensory mode questionnaire or the HBDI with each group you give instruction to. However, you can assume that there are likely to be people from each type of brain dominance and sensory preference in your group. So, in order to give them all an opportunity of learning in the most effective way, you should include in your lesson elements which cover as wide a range of activities as possible.

Multiple intelligences

Another useful concept which can have an important impact on training is that of multiple intelligences. In his book *Frames of Mind*[5] Howard Gardner, Professor of Education at Harvard University described research which showed that intelligence can be defined in other ways than by the traditional logical/mathematical and linguistic IQ tests. He identified seven intelligences:

1 **The linguistic intelligence**. Skill with words, as exemplified by writers, public speakers and negotiators.
2 **The mathematical/logical intelligence**. Skill in analysis and logic, as exemplified by scientists, economists, mathematicians and statisticians.
3 **The visual/spatial intelligence**.The ability to visualize and create images in your mind's eye, as exemplified by architects, navigators, artists and photographers.
4 **The musical intelligence**. The ability to create and identify complex patterns of sound, as exemplified by musicians, composers and lovers of classical music.
5 **The kinesthetic intelligence**. The ability to use the body skilfully, as exemplified by surgeons, athletes, dancers and people who are 'good with their hands'.
6 **The inter-personal intelligence**. The ability to communicate well, as exemplified by salespeople, gifted trainers and some parents.
7 **The intra-personal intelligence**. The ability to create one's own goals and plans, to be reflective, to analyse one's behaviour as a guide to future action.

People whose natural preference is to rely more on the third to the seventh of the above intelligences are often dismissed as poor learners. What is worse, they may think of themselves as such. As a trainer you can do much to help them by making them aware of their strengths in other forms of intelligence and by including in your lessons activities which give them an opportunity of learning in a way which suits them.

In the book *The Learning Revolution*[6] there is a full description of the seven intelligences, together with a description of likely traits and how to strengthen those intelligences for learning. Let us look at how a training session might be organized for a group which contains different types of learners (as, in reality, do all groups).

Let us assume that Mary Weller wants to give a training session to a group of clerks in the accounting department on the financing of export trade. She has assessed her own brain dominance pattern and is shown as being lower right (humanistic/emotional), with a preference for visual information processing. She believes that in the group the majority are either lower-left or upper-left quadrant dominant (i.e., left brained). One person, however, is probably upper right quadrant dominant (future-oriented, i.e., right-brained).

The aim of the lesson is to interest the staff in the subject and to give them an overview of the main methods of financing an export transaction. To give a balanced presentation Mary needs, if possible, to incorporate the following elements.

For the practical left-brained learners she should make it clear what the aim of the lesson is and how it fits into their long-term company goals. This means giving an introductory talk to explain the importance of export financing for the future export business of the company and possibly in the participants' future careers. She should explain the application of any theoretical knowledge she gives them.

She should start and finish on time and stick to a well-organized lesson plan. She should help the participants to develop their imagination,

Figure 8.2 ... *she should start and finish on time and stick to a well-organized lesson plan ...*

something they probably find quite difficult. She might do this by giving them a short guided visualization exercise. They probably need help, too, in working with others, so she should consider what group activities might achieve this.

For the right-brained learners she should show the total picture, including an overview of the lesson. To appeal to their imaginations she might act out a dialogue, either with puppets or with a volunteer rehearsed in advance. She might also give a guided visualization, perhaps of the country from which the export order was received. She should work in an unhurried way and present her material in an artistically appealing manner.

To help with the right-brained learners' area of weakness she should insist on attention to detail, ask them to examine ideas critically, carry out energy raising exercises when energy or interest flags and not allow them to be distracted.

Mary will also need to take account of differences in the preferred sensory modes of the people in the group.

For the visual learners: She should prepare and use OHP transparencies, flip charts and other visual aids, such as video, 35mm projectors and wall charts. She should encourage visualization.

For the auditory learners: She should give verbal explanations, using the full range of pitch and volume of her voice. She might consider the use of tape-recorded voices, music and sound effects.

For the kinesthetic learners: She should present plenty of opportunities for physical movement, introduce role plays, discussions, games, etc.

Finally, she needs to take account of her own brain dominance and not allow it to upset the balance of the lesson.

Exercise   You are about to run a one-week course for a group of 15 senior managers on a subject in which you are an expert.

You have had an opportunity of conducting the Herrmann Brain Dominance Instrument with them in advance. Their group profile is shown in Figure 8.3.

Prepare a lesson plan on a subject familiar to you, analysing it as above, with activities for learners from all four brain dominance quadrants.

Notes and references   1 The Herrmann Brain Dominance Instrument (HBDI) is available in the UK from The Ned Herrmann Group (UK), see Appendix D for address. They will supply the profile questionnaire on request and will mark it when you return it to them. They then provide you with a detailed, illustrated report on your brain dominance and preferred thinking style, at a cost of about £35.

Group composite # 2

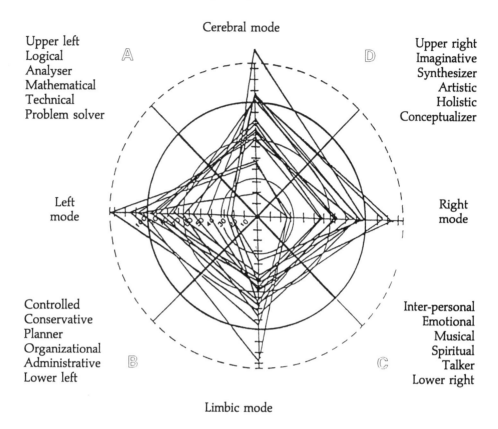

Cerebral mode

Upper left
Logical
Analyser
Mathematical
Technical
Problem solver

Ⓐ

Ⓓ

Upper right
Imaginative
Synthesizer
Artistic
Holistic
Conceptualizer

Left
mode

Right
mode

Controlled
Conservative
Planner
Organizational
Administrative
Lower left

Ⓑ

Ⓒ

Inter-personal
Emotional
Musical
Spiritual
Talker
Lower right

Limbic mode

Figure 8.3 *Herrmann Brain Dominance Profile. Group composite # 2 © 1986, Ned Herrmann*

2 The Hemisphere Centre Profile (HCP) test was developed by David Loye. It is to be found in Loye, D. (1983) *The Sphinx and the Rainbow* (pp. 176–177), New Science Library/SHAMBHALA, Boulder and London and Shambhala Publications, Colorado. The test takes about three minutes to complete. It is a simple but effective way of helping people to understand whether they are likely to be left- or right-brain dominant.

3 The Brain Map, otherwise known as the DolphinThink Self-Assessment Profile, is produced by the Brain Technologies Corporation, Colorado USA. It makes four basic thinking style classifications, based on left/right and posterior/anterior brain quadrants. These are 'I-Control' (The Organizer, The Analyser, The Fine Print Expert); 'I-Pursue' (The Competitor, The Doer, The Super-Achiever); 'I-Preserve' (The Belonger, The Believer, The Guardian); and 'I-Explore' (The Visionary, The Creator, The Searcher). It is available in the UK from Management Learning Resources Ltd., PO Box 28, Carmarthen, Dyfed SA31 1DT. It is supplied as a booklet with complete instructions for self-marking and costs about £10.

4 The Personal Thinking Style test was developed by Professor Anthony Gregorc, Professor of Curriculum and Instruction at the University of Connecticut. It shows how a person processes information, and classifies thinkers into four categories: Concrete Sequential, Abstract Sequential, Abstract Random and Concrete Random. It is explained in full in the following two books: De Porter, B. (1993) *Quantum Learning* (pp. 126–142), Piatkus Books, London, and Dryden, G. and Voss, J. (1993) *The Learning Revolution* (pp. 355–359), Profile Books, Auckland, New Zealand. The latter is available from Accelerated Learning Systems Ltd. (see Appendix D for address).

5 Gardner, H. (1983) *Frames of Mind—The Theory of Multiple Intelligences*, Paladin, London.

6 Dryden, G. and Voss, J. op. cit. Chapter 10.

Sit in a chair with your feet together on the floor in front of you and your back straight, either unsupported or resting lightly against an upright chair back. Place the palms of your hands on either side of your ribs, just below your armpits. Breathe in so that your ribs expand outwards, pushing your hands out to the side. Inhale and exhale several times. In this way you are filling the middle of your lungs with air.

Now place the palms of your hands on your abdomen, with the tips of your fingers just touching. Let your abdomen go slack and breathe in. Allow the incoming breath to cause a slight expansion of the abdomen. You may notice a slight separation of your fingers. Imagine that the abdomen is a balloon being slowly inflated. Breathe out deeply and feel your fingers coming together and the abdomen contracting. Continue for at least six breaths.

Now combine the two types of breathing. Start with the expansion of the ribs and continue with the abdomen. After a while you will not need your hands to guide the process.

Put a finger on your pulse and count the beats, becoming aware of the rate. Using the pulse frequency as a guide, breathe in to the count of four. Hold the breath for a four-count and breathe out for a four-count. Continue this breath pattern of 4-4-4.

There are many variations to this practice. As you become more experienced you can lengthen the period of retention and exhalation of the breath, so that the pattern might become: in 4-hold 8-out 8. The retention of the breath for longer periods allows more oxygen to be transferred to the blood and hence to the brain. Slowing down the out-breath has a heightened mind-calming effect.

Relaxation

Relaxation is a skill which has to be learned. It is fundamental to the management of stress and it also creates a condition which is ideal for learning and visualization. In this state the electrical waves of the brain slow down to a frequency (about 12 hertz) known as alpha. This state can be induced by certain types of music, notably the largo and adagio passages from Baroque compositions. An alternative, which is more effective for some people, is to practise muscular and mental relaxation exercises drawn from the Jacobson method, Autogenic Training or Yoga. There are a great many of these exercises and the following is a short selection.

The Jacobson Method

Make a fist with the right hand and hold it tense while you count up to six. Relax the hand and notice the difference in sensation. Press the palm of the right hand onto the right knee and bring the right arm under tension. Hold the tension for the count of six and relax the arm. Notice the difference. Curl the toes of the right foot and bring the foot under tension. Hold and relax. Turn the foot up and bring the shin muscles under tension. Hold and relax. Press down on the right foot and bring the right leg under tension. Hold and relax.

Repeat the same tensing and relaxing exercises with the left side of the body.

Tense the stomach muscles, hold and relax.

Raise the shoulders, hold them tensed and relax.

Make a grimace and hold the tension in the muscles of the face. Hold and relax.

Tense all the muscles previously worked on. Hold the whole body in a state of tension. Relax. Allow a wave of relaxation to flow over the whole body.

Autogenic Training

Imagine a feeling of heaviness in your right arm. Say to yourself several times: My right arm is heavy. Keep practising this for several days or until you detect a distinct sensation of heaviness in the right arm. Then do the same with the left arm, followed by each of the legs. The exercise is cumulative, that is you always start with the right arm and add each limb successively until they have all been visualized together as heavy.

Imagine a feeling of warmth in your right hand. Feel it spreading up the arm. Say to yourself: My right arm is warm. Follow the same procedure as above for heaviness.

Become aware of your heartbeat and say to yourself: My heartbeat is calm and regular.

Become aware of your breathing and say to yourself: It breathes me.

This is a very abbreviated description of some of the Autogenic Training exercises. For a full description see Dr Kai Kermani's book *Autogenic Training*.[1] Better still, find a qualified teacher and take lessons. You can obtain a list of teachers from the British Association for Autogenic Training.[2]

Yoga

Focus your attention on the thumb of your right hand. Become fully aware of it. Do not move it, but simply allow any tension to slip away. Move your attention to the fingers of your right hand, each one in turn.

Focus for a moment on each of the following parts of the body (on the right side): forearm, elbow, shoulder, armpit, rib cage, hip, thigh, buttock, knee, calf, heel, sole of the foot, big toe and each of the remaining toes in turn.

Repeat for the same parts on the left side of the body.

Become aware in turn of the abdomen, chest, throat, chin, mouth, nose, eyes, forehead, ears and crown of the head.

Again, this is a very condensed version of what is known as Yoga Nidra. For a full description, refer to the book *Yoga Nidra* by Swami Satyananda Saraswati.[3] Another book which contains detailed guidance on yoga postures which can be carried out in the office is called Office Yoga.[4]

To find a qualified Yoga teacher in your area, contact the British Wheel of Yoga.[5]

Emotional calmness

The next requirement for the optimum functioning of the brain is emotional calmness. Anyone who has tried to learn or think creatively while they are feeling angry, excited, worried or depressed will know that concentration on the task is difficult, if not impossible. One solution is to visualize objects or scenes which are by their nature peaceful. In this way the disturbing mental images are replaced by calming ones and the emotional state gradually changes.

Some objects or scenes which can be visualized are: the sky at night, a red sky at sunset, birds flying across clouds, a deserted beach, an endless desert, snow-capped mountains, any quiet, peaceful scene from the natural world.

Alternatively, you can use guided visualization to take the group on a peaceful walk in a forest, around a garden, up a mountain, along a beach or any other peaceful place that you can describe in multi-sensory detail (see Chapter 13, Visualization).

Concentration

None of the mental and physical activities described above will serve their purpose, particularly if the aim is to prepare for learning, without the skill of concentration. The mind has an almost irresistible tendency to wander and it is only by constant practice that one can learn to keep it on one subject for any length of time. The following are some exercises to help course participants to improve their power of concentration. Although the exercises can be taught at a seminar they can only be learned by the individual through sustained and regular practice.

Fixing the attention on the breath

Focus your attention on the breath, at the point where it enters and leaves the nostrils. Be aware of the difference in temperature as it enters and leaves. If your thoughts wander, bring them gently back to the breath. Do this for a minute to start with and gradually increase the time to ten minutes or longer. This form of concentration is particularly suitable for people with a dominant kinesthetic sense (see Chapter 8).

Gazing at a candle

Fix your gaze on a candle flame and hold it, without blinking, for as long as possible. After a few minutes, close your eyes and observe the after-image of the flame on the dark space behind your closed eyelids. Look at the flame again and repeat the exercise. This form of concentration is particularly suitable for people with a dominant visual sense.

Repeating a sound   Choose a syllable or word, such as 'OM' or 'Peace' or 'One', and repeat it silently, without allowing any other thoughts to intrude. This form of concentration is the basis of Transcendental Meditation (TM).[6] It is particularly suitable for people with a dominant auditory sense.

Energy

Gaining access to the reserve powers of the brain means becoming aware of the interconnection between the brain and the body of which it is an integral part. The optimum functioning of the whole brain depends on the maintenance of a high level of energy in the body. The energy level of the body changes considerably throughout the day and this affects the functioning of the brain. It is a useful exercise to ask the members of your group to plot their energy level at various times in the day in order to make them aware of the way it varies. Appendix C contains a chart for this purpose.

Before starting a training session it is worthwhile assessing the energy level of the group and, if necessary, taking steps to adjust it. If the level is too high, as might be the case after a stressful car journey or a confrontational meeting, it may be desirable to lower it by slow, deep breathing and relaxation exercises. If it is too low, as will often be the case when the whole day is spent sitting in an office or a lecture room, it may be necessary to raise it. This can be done by a number of exercises, all of them involving physical movement and/or deep breathing.

A number of useful exercises can be borrowed from Educational Kinesiology (Brain Gym).[7] They have the additional advantage of activating certain areas of the brain for specific mental activities, such as reading or writing. Three particularly useful exercises for raising energy and connecting the left and right brain are:

1 **The cross crawl**. Stand with feet apart, raise the left knee and touch it with the right hand. Then raise the right knee and touch it with the left hand. Repeat, alternating rhythmically and if necessary speeding up and hopping between hand position changes. Some lively music will raise energy levels still further.
2 **Brain buttons**. Press the forefinger and middle finger of the left hand against the navel and with the thumb, forefinger and middle finger of the other hand rub deeply just below the collarbone, to the right and left of the sternum.
3 **Arm activation**. Raise one arm above the head and hold it next to the ear. Exhale gently through pursed lips while activating the

muscles by pushing the arm against the other hand in four directions (front, back, in and away).

Some 30 such exercises are listed in the book *Brain Gym*, available from the Hendon Natural Health Centre,[8] but they are best carried out after attending a course, when their full significance will be appreciated. Courses are run by a number of qualified EduK (Educational Kinesiology) teachers throughout the UK and their names can be obtained from the Hendon Centre.

Life style

It is not possible for the brain to work properly if the body is not in good health and functioning efficiently. This means regular exercise, plenty of fresh air, sufficient undisturbed sleep and a sensible diet.

A sensible diet is, above all, a moderate one. It is difficult to maintain full mental awareness and concentration after a heavy meal, as the blood needed for the brain is diverted to the stomach to aid digestion. It also means choosing the right kind of food and avoiding food which reduces vitality and is harmful to health. The World Health Organisation (WHO) in a report entitled *Diet, Nutrition and the Prevention of Chronic Disease* (1991) recommended the following foods:

- **Fruit, vegetables and salads**. Eat as much as you like; they are low in calories but high in fibre, vitamins and minerals.
- **Bread and cereals (particularly wholemeal) and potatoes**. Satisfy your appetite; they give you fibre, vitamins and a variety of minerals.
- **Meat, fish and dairy products**. You can eat moderate amounts of lean meat and white fish but keep the level of fat intake low. Avoid saturated fats, such as are found in pies, burgers and sausages. They cause blood cholesterol levels to rise which is a risk factor in heart disease.

Foods to avoid are: processed foods, biscuits and foods which contain harmful additives or too much sugar, salt or fat.

Combining foods correctly is also important, so that the digestive process is not overloaded. A book which describes this well and which gives sensible advice about what and how to eat without becoming hungry is *Fit for Life*.[9] One of its main recommendations is to eat only fruit in the morning, so that the digestive process from the previous day can be completed. Another is to avoid combining in the same meal high protein foods, such as meat and eggs, with carbohydrates, such as bread, rice or potatoes.

Most books on diet also recommend cutting down on caffeine-based drinks, such as coffee, teas and colas. Alcohol in moderate amounts (wine, not spirits) is not harmful, but if you are drinking more than three glasses of wine a day or their equivalent (two if you are a woman) you may be approaching the limits of your body's tolerance.

Smoking is now almost universally condemned by authorities on health and diet. It clogs up your lungs so that you cannot breathe deeply or enjoy the exercise you need. It also exposes you and those around you to the risk of cancer and heart disease. As a trainer you have a responsibility to insist that smokers refrain from smoking in seminar rooms. Most of them accept this ruling without demur, but it often needs to be made clear at the beginning of a training session.

To sum up, the effectiveness of your training sessions can be increased enormously if you are aware of the way that mental processes are linked to what is going on in the body. Stress interferes with learning. So does low energy. You have a responsibility to help your course participants get the most out of their training with you. Now you know how to go about it.

Notes and references

1 Kermani, K. (1990) *Autogenic Training*, Souvenir Press, London.
2 The British Association for Autogenic Training, 101 Harley Street, London W1.
3 Saraswati, S. S. (1982) *Yoga Nidra*, Bihar School of Yoga, Monghyr, India. This book is available from Satyananda Yoga Centre, 70 Thurleigh Road, London SW12 8UD.
4 Friedberger, J. (1991) *Office Yoga*, Thorsons Publishing Group, Wellingborough.
5 British Wheel of Yoga, 1 Hamilton Place, Boston Road, Sleaford, Lincs NG34 7ES.
6 Transcendental Meditation, Roydon Hall, East Peckham, Nr. Tonbridge, Kent TN12 5NH.
7 Brain Gym: Details of courses and books can be obtained from the Hendon Natural Health Centre, 12 Golders Rise, London NW4 2HR.
8 Dennison, P. and Dennison, G. (1996) *Brain Gym—Instant Brain Boosters for On-the-Job Success*, Edu-Kinesthetics Inc., Ventura, California.
9 Diamond, H. and Diamond, M. (1985) *Fit for Life*, Bantam Press, London.

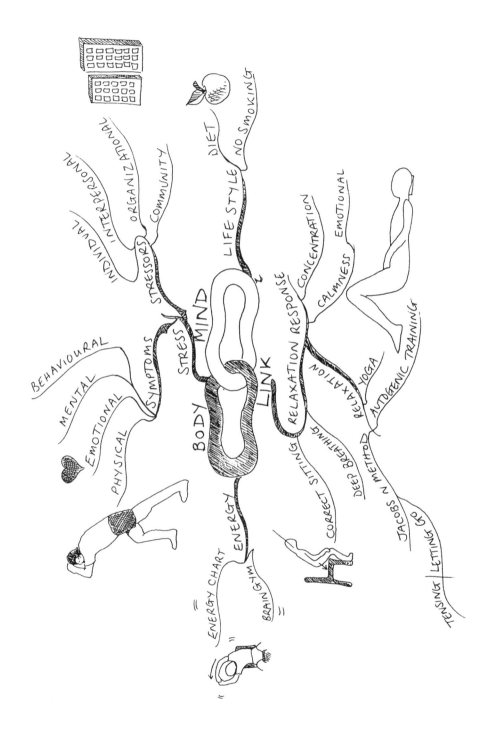

Mind map for Chapter 9—body–mind link

10 Suggestion

The more faithfully you listen to the voice within you, the better you will hear what is sounding outside

Dag Hammarskjold

Scene *The reception show room at Glospot Ltd. The group of 20 newly-recruited moulding shop operatives were clearly nervous. All of them were women, many of them returning to work after bringing up a family, and they were apprehensive about their ability to learn a new skill. They sat in the spacious show room cum lecture room, ill at ease, many of them smoking nervously.*

'I don't know why I've come here,' whispered Maureen, a ruddy-faced mature woman to her neighbour, Jenny, a small woman with a mournful expression.

'Me neither,' replied Jenny. 'I don't know how I passed the interview. I feel as if I don't know anything. Not after 20 years bringing up the kids. Stopped learning at 16, I did. Didn't know much then, either. I doubt if I'd ever be able to make a pot like that. Beautiful, isn't it?'

She pointed to one of several large colour photographs of pots made by the company. They were indeed fine examples of the potter's art—deep, multi-hued glazes and artistic designs. There were also other pictures showing the development of the company and its export markets. They noticed as they looked around that the room had other pleasant features. There were bunches of cut flowers in vases at the tables and there was some soft background music of the sixties and seventies playing.

They looked up as a man came into the room. It was Tony Wakeman. He was dressed in a well-cut suit with a discreet check pattern and a brightly coloured tie. He exuded confidence and friendliness as he stood in front of them, arms at his sides and body poised, his weight distributed evenly on both feet. The women sat up and hastily put out their cigarettes.

'Good morning, everyone,' said Tony cheerfully, looking around the room and making eye contact with each person in turn. His voice was pleasant and well-modulated and had a ring of authority.

'My name is Tony Wakeman and I'm attached to Glospot as a training consultant. I'd like to welcome you and to say how delighted we are to have you as part of our workforce. We are particularly pleased that there are so many of you who are returning to work after a career break. We have found that people in this position are usually well-motivated and eager to learn. We aim to build a mutually-supportive learning environment in which you will find learning about moulding interesting and enjoyable.'

Maureen and Jenny exchanged glances and smiled. Perhaps going back to work would not be so terrifying after all.

The concept of suggestion in learning lies at the heart of Suggestopedia, the method from which Accelerated Learning is derived. Dr Lozanov, the creator of the method, developed Suggestopedia[1] to demonstrate that the reserve powers of the brain, which lie in the subconscious, can be accessed by the use of suggestion. This indirect route to the reserve powers has to be used because the mind contains certain barriers—emotional, logical and ethical—which prevent suggestion from entering directly into the subconscious. Lozanov called this De-suggestion.

These barriers may present an obstacle to developing an individual's potential, because they prevent him or her from accepting that development is possible. Most people have been conditioned by their home or school environment to believe that their memory, their creativity and their overall ability are limited. They accept the label given to them as children and are unable to imagine themselves being different.

This can be a serious impediment to retraining staff in a company or to helping people facing redundancy to find a new role. It can also represent a ceiling for an able employee who does not consider him or herself capable of accepting promotion. So the trainer has to de-suggest the negative concepts embedded in the subconscious minds of the learners and substitute positive beliefs through suggestion. There follow some ways of doing this.

Double-planeness

Double- or dual-planeness is a concept used by Lozanov to explain the influence of messages transmitted and received below the conscious level or plane. As far as the trainer is concerned, this is mainly a matter of non-verbal communication—facial expression, posture, gesture and tone of voice. This is covered in more detail below under the heading 'Authority'. The environment can also contain dual plane messages. These messages contain considerable information. They are the source of intuitive impressions which form attitudes.

Purposeful employment of this second plane of behaviour begins to inspire confidence and allows positive suggestion to become effective. The role of the trainer is similar to that of an actor, but it is essential that he or she is sincere.

Double-planeness, according to Lozanov, is 'the stream of diverse stimuli which, consciously or unconsciously, are emitted from or perceived by an individual'. This concept has been developed to a high degree in Neuro-Linguistic Programming.[2] Some of the key NLP principles which reflect the concept of double-planeness are:

1 **Sensory acuity**. Being aware of the reaction of students to the message one is sending them. 'The meaning of the communication is the response that you get' is a key NLP concept. The responses are often non-verbal and go unnoticed without careful observation. The trainer keeps on changing the form of communication until the message receives a favourable response on the behavioural level.
2 **Rapport**. Building trust on a non-verbal level by 'pacing' (discreet mirroring of another person's posture, movements and voice) and 'leading' (changing your behaviour so that the other person follows).
3 **Observing eye movements and body language**. Becoming aware of mismatches in communication. For example, a trainer who relies a great deal on visual presentations may notice that some members of the class are becoming restive. He realizes that they may be kinesthetic learners, so he involves them in some physical activity, such as creating a mind map or having a group discussion. He adapts the presentation to suit their learning style.

Authority

Authority in this context means, in the words of Lozanov, non-directive prestige. It does not mean being authoritarian. It creates an atmosphere of confidence and intuitive desire to follow the example of the trainer. There is a feeling that the information being conveyed is reliable and authentic and that it is worth learning.

Two ways in which a trainer can convey authority are by the use of the voice and of the body. Both can be learned through the Alexander Technique. This teaches poised, deliberate movements of the body and a harmonious use of the voice (see Chapter 11). If we think of people we know who exhibit authority in the sense referred to here, we usually find that they move in a poised, deliberate way. Their posture is balanced and they do not make nervous gestures. They exhibit an inner calm. They give eye contact. They speak in measured tones. Their voice tends to be low pitched but with variety of intonation. Margaret Thatcher, for instance, took lessons in lowering the pitch of her voice, in order to increase her effectiveness on television.

All these qualities can be acquired through the Alexander Technique.[3] This teaches poise, self-awareness and the ability to control and direct the movements of the body. Actions are accomplished in a natural way and with the minimum of effort. The technique also teaches voice production, so that pitch, volume and pace are varied, pauses are introduced and what is said is listened to with attention (see Chapter 11).

Lozanov compares the suggestopedic teacher to an accomplished actor, using their body and voice to convey dual-plane messages of authority and positive suggestion. Acting ability is another desirable quality of the Accelerated Learning trainer. It can be used in a variety of ways, in addition to the creation of authority. One of them is to introduce or illustrate a subject by means of a sketch, which can be in the form of a dialogue or monologue. This can awaken interest and is particularly effective with right-brain dominant learners, who like human interest and humour. Another is to use glove puppets.

Most trainers could learn the basic skills of acting. One way of acquiring them is to attend the weekend 'Mastery' course at the Actors Institute (see Appendix D for address).

Environment

The classroom environment can have an important influence on the subconscious attitude to learning. Bright colours, pictures, flowers, music, comfortable chairs in a circle all suggest a pleasant, relaxing experience. This creates an atmosphere of enjoyment and overcomes barriers based on previous negative experience (see Chapter 4).

Concert state

Lozanov found, by experiment, that the ability to memorize was enhanced considerably if learners entered a state of relaxed awareness. In this state the brain waves slow down to a frequency of between about 8 and 12 cycles a second. This is known as the alpha state. This state can be induced by relaxation exercises, based for example on Yoga or Autogenic Training or by playing slow movements (largo and adagio) from Baroque music.

In the concert session the material that is to be learned is read by the trainer, accompanied by Baroque music (see Chapter 5). The trainer reads the text in a quiet voice, varying volume, pitch and intonation to take into account the features of the music. The combination of voice and body language should convey a feeling of conviction and of the importance of the meaning of the text.

This concert reading can be given at the beginning of the lesson or at the end in the form of a review. The 'review concert' is more common in training applications, as opposed to language tuition, when it comes at the beginning. It produces a relaxed, confident attitude towards the material being presented, similar to that when attending a genuine concert. The listeners are behaviourally passive and make no intellectual effort to memorize or understand. In this state the anti-suggestive barriers are overcome and the reserve capacities of the mind are released.

As already mentioned, the state of relaxed awareness can be induced by other means. Two of the best known are Autogenic Training and Yoga Nidra (see Chapter 9). Furthermore, music other than Baroque can be used to enhance the alpha state (see Chapter 4, Music). It should be born in mind by trainers that a concert session or one using the relaxation techniques described above, can have a highly beneficial effect on a therapeutic level. It can relax the body, calm the mind, overcome fatigue and give fresh energy. The relaxation skills learned can be used by individuals to overcome stress in their lives.

The inner child

It is well known that the child can memorize much more information than the adult. The adult's memory and imagination weaken in inverse proportion to the growth of reasoning. At the same time, a social norm is established, not only for the lack of importance of memory, but for an individual's limited capacity to memorize. This suggestive norm becomes a barrier, which must first be removed by a process of de-suggestion.

This process of de-suggestion can be assisted considerably by getting in touch with the child which every adult has within. Techniques for getting in touch with the inner child include:

- The display of works of art. These activate the affective and intuitive parts of the brain.
- A serene attitude on the part of the teacher towards the process of teaching.
- The playing of roles and the allocation of fictitious identities. These liberate students from their social positions and facilitate the removal of anti-suggestive barriers.
- Singing or playing games. These assist memory, promote a positive group dynamic and help participants to get in touch with their inner child.

The concept of the inner child—Lozanov calls it Infantilization—is perhaps the most difficult of the suggestopedic principles to introduce into company training. Adult learners, particularly senior managers, who are used to sitting theatre style and being taught by means of a lecture and OHP, are likely to be resistant to a method which moves them out of their seats and behaving in ways which they may perceive as undignified.

To overcome this resistance the company trainer would be wise to explain the rationale before any games or similar activities are introduced. This can be done verbally at the start of the course or by means of a description of the method in the course joining instructions. If the logical, critical barriers of the participants are thus addressed in advance, there may be a willingness to at least try the new activities. Thereafter it is up to the trainer to lead by example and to show that learning is taking place.

There is less resistance to this kind of activity than there used to be, mainly because of the increasing popularity of outdoor management training and action learning. There are several books describing classroom activities and 'ice-breakers', which involve behaviour which is essentially childlike and which is accepted willingly by most trainees. Examples are given in Chapters 6 and 7.

The group dynamic also plays an important role in this process. By working harmoniously together, the group gains a feeling of growing confidence and an expectation that the programme will be pleasant and enjoyable.

Language

It is important that all language used by the trainer is framed in positive terms. Criticism is avoided and encouragement emphasized. There are many techniques from NLP which can be used effectively in this context. One of them is to express information in positive as opposed to negative terms. For example, instead of saying 'You will not find producing mouldings difficult' (a sentence which contains two negative words), Tony might say 'You will find making mouldings easy—rather like the way you make a jelly in a mould for a birthday party'.

Another approach is to use so-called 'embedded commands'. Instead of saying 'I want you all to relax and feel at home here', Tony might say 'You may find it takes you a little time to relax and feel at home here'. There are many other examples of this kind from NLP, some of which are described in the book *Trance-formations*[4] and in the two books on NLP mentioned in note 2.

It is worthwhile examining the language you use in your training sessions and making sure that what you say is framed in positive and not negative terms. You can usually get an idea of the effect that your words are having by carefully observing the facial expressions and body language of your audience.

Visualization and affirmation

Another important aspect of suggestion is the use of affirmation and visualization. These two techniques can, with practice, place the power of suggestion in the hands of the learner and make them independent of the trainer. Once a student has learned how to visualize clearly, they can use the technique to build self-esteem, get in touch with 'resourceful states' (experiences of past successes) and create a clear and believable picture of future success. If these pictures are accompanied by positive verbal affirmations, they can create an expectation of successful learning achievement and can become highly motivating (see Chapter 13 for guidance on visualization techniques).

The concept of the resourceful state is drawn from NLP. Accelerated Learning trainers would be well-advised to take some training in this method. Details of courses can be obtained from the Association of Neuro-Linguistic Training, 48 Corser Street, Stourbridge DY8 2DQ, Telephone: 0384 443935.

To sum up, trainers can considerably enhance their effectiveness in the classroom by an awareness of the untapped mental reserves in their students or trainees and the ways in which their use of suggestion can help these reserves to be accessed.

Notes and references

1 Lozanov, G. (1978) *Suggestology and Outlines of Suggestopody* (Chapter 4), Gordon and Breach Science Publishers, London. The concept is described fully in this chapter. The publisher can be contacted at 42 IV Street, London WC2 4DE.
2 O'Connor, J. and Seymour, J. (1993) Introducing Neuro-Linguistic Programming (pp. 19–23), Aquarian Press, Wellingborough; and O'Connor, J. and Seymour, J. (1994) *Training with NLP* (pp. 126–209).
3 For a description of the Alexander Technique, refer to the following books: Hodgkinson, L. and Piatkus, J. (1988) *The Alexander Technique and how it can help you*, Piatkus Books, London; Gelb, M. (1981) *Body learning—An introduction to the Alexander Technique*, Aurum Press, London; and Barlow, W. (1973) *The Alexander Principle*, Arrow Books, London.
4 Bandler, R. and Grinder, J. (1981) *Trance-formations*, Real People Press, Moab, Utah USA.

Mind map for Chapter 10—suggestion

11 Voice production and body movement

If you want a quality, act as if you already had it. Try the 'As If' technique

William James

Scene *The training room at Glospot Ltd. Roger Martin, the moulding shop manager, was a large man of about 50, with an anxious expression and wispy, greying hair. As he came into the training room he did not look at the group of 15 moulding shop operators assembled for a lesson on the new German press which the company had just bought. He hurried over to the table at the end of the room, his head bent forward and his eyes on the floor. His mouth was firmly shut in an expression of severity. He switched on the OHP and placed a foil on it. The words DEMAG PRESS appeared on the large white screen.*

'Right,' said Roger, in a high, nervous voice. 'This is a lesson on the new DEMAG hydraulic press. Listen carefully, because I'm not going to repeat myself. Anyone who loses a finger while operating it will have only themselves to blame.' As he said this he looked severely at his audience. It was the first time he had given them eye contact. He hastily looked back at his notes. Several people in the audience crossed their legs and folded their arms.

When the lesson was over, Tony Wakeman, who had been making a video recording, invited Roger to stay behind and have a look at extracts from the video playback. It was the first time Roger had seen himself on video and he was visibly shaken at what he saw.

'Do I really look like that?' he asked, his voice sounding highly uncomfortable.

'I'm afraid so,' replied Tony. 'But cheer up. The main thing is that you seem to recognize that there's room for improvement. And the good news is that there's a way to help you. It's called the Alexander Technique. I can teach you the basics of it in an hour or so. If you're willing to practise there's no reason why you shouldn't become an effective public speaker.'

'To tell you the truth,' said Roger, 'I hate it. I hate getting up in front of an audience. I've always been scared stiff of it. I suppose I cover it up by looking severe.'

'That's not uncommon,' said Tony. 'Most people are nervous about speaking before an audience. I used to be terrified. The secret is to act as if you feel confident. The audience won't know what's going on inside you. And if you act confident then you gradually start to actually feel confident. How would you hold yourself if you felt confident?'

'Well, I suppose I'd stand up straight and look at the audience a bit more. I might even smile sometimes.'

'Exactly. Well, you can learn to do both. If you want to get your posture right, just remember a simple rule: "Head forward and up". Then everything else falls into place. There are a few other things to bear in mind, like standing still, breathing deeply, projecting your voice and allowing pauses. But there's no mystery about them. Would you like a lesson?'

'I certainly would,' replied Roger, fervently. 'When can we start?'

As already mentioned in the first chapter, as trainers we are often unaware of the powerful influence we exert by the way we use our body and our voice. Both convey messages on the subconscious level. It is impossible for us not to communicate with them, quite regardless of the content of what we are teaching.

In a well-known study, the American psychologist Robert Mehrabian reported that the following factors influenced communication in the proportions shown:

Body language (i.e. facial expression, gesture, posture, etc.)—55%
Voice (i.e. tone, stress, pitch, pauses, use of silence, etc.)—38%
Verbal content (i.e. words alone)—7%

Most trainers concentrate their attention on what they have to say, that is, on the verbal content of their lesson. Very few think about the way they say it or the use they make of their body while they are saying it. The result is that, although what they say may be understood, it will not be remembered. This is because it has not penetrated the so-called logical/critical and emotional barriers of their listeners. We all have mental barriers which protect our minds from the surfeit of useless information which we are exposed to every day of our lives. If we did not have them we would become totally confused.

If the information we are receiving comes from a source which is lacking in authority or which has a negative emotion connected to it, we will tend to reject it on a subconscious level and not allow it to go in to our long-term memory. So, if a trainer like Roger comes into a classroom the subconscious barriers in the minds of the students will effectively prevent learning taking place.

So what can we do about it? If we are feeling depressed is it not more honest to let our bodies reflect our feelings and perhaps to tell our students about our problems? There is an argument in support of doing this. It may make us more human in the eyes of our students and perhaps create rapport with them. *But* there is a heavy price to pay for such honesty. The negative energy which we bring with us, and expect our class to share, will soon communicate itself to them and lower their enthusiasm for whatever it is we want to teach. No one likes to be in the company of someone who is in a negative frame of mind. There is much truth in the saying 'Laugh and the world laughs with you. Cry and you cry alone'.

The truth is that a successful trainer has to be something of an actor. A good actor will never allow personal feelings to interfere with the interpretation of a role. The audience would never stand for it if he did. He has to think himself into the emotional state of the part he is playing. A trainer who wishes to give a successful lesson must do the same. He must consciously take control of his body movements and voice and use them to convey a message of enthusiasm and cheerfulness. Only in this way will he win the attention and cooperation of his class.

Let us look at how one can do this, taking the use of the body first.

Use of the body

The first step is to be aware of the way in which one is using one's body and the effect this is having both on the people one is teaching and on one's own emotional state. If Roger had paused for a moment and realized how he was holding himself with head lowered, eyes cast down and with a grim expression on his face, he would have become aware of the effect this was producing on the class. He might also have realized how his body posture was reinforcing his pattern of negative thinking.

Having brought the attention inwards for a moment from the outside world, the next step is to take charge of one's body and consciously to direct its movements and posture. There is such a thing as 'good use' of the body. Unfortunately, it is something that most adults have forgotten, even though they may have followed its rules spontaneously as children. Good use is a matter of balance and the avoidance of unnecessary tension. If we allow our head to fall forward or jerk back, if we cross our legs when we sit down, if we fold our arms, if we stand habitually on one leg, or if we lie with twisted limbs and curved spine, we are destroying the natural balance of the body. This lack of balance in the body will contribute towards a lack of centredness and poise in the mind. It will also produce muscular tension which will eventually cause pain.

The Alexander Technique[1]

One of the best methods for acquiring good use of the body and the mental poise and authority which it brings with it is the Alexander Technique. This was invented by an Australian actor called Mathias Alexander, who was born in Tasmania in 1869 and died in London in 1955. As a young man he became renowned for his brilliant recitals of Shakespeare. At the height of his career, however, he began to lose the strength and timbre which made his voice so attractive. He was unable to find a doctor who could help him recover the quality of his voice, so he looked for a cure himself. He discovered, by observing himself in a mirror, that he jerked his head backwards slightly whenever he started to recite. By consciously directing his head forwards and upwards, he found that the quality of his voice was restored. This was due to the releasing of the tension in the larynx which the regular pulling back of the head had caused.

Alexander discovered that by directing his head forwards and upwards he was doing much more than just improving the quality of his voice. The quality of use of his whole body also improved quite markedly. He became more poised. Muscular pain became less frequent, particularly in his back. Furthermore, he experienced an inner sense of calmness and centredness. He moved and spoke with increased authority.

Soon he was giving lessons in the use of the body and the voice and he gave up his stage career to concentrate on teaching the technique which was to bear his name. He moved to England and became a well-known figure, teaching such eminent people as Aldous Huxley and George Bernard Shaw.

The only way to learn the Alexander Technique properly is to have individual lessons with a qualified teacher. However, a number of books have been written about it so there are undoubtedly some aspects of the method which can help people to improve the use of their body, even without taking a full course. The following are some general guidelines and the terms by which they are known.

Good use

This is, as mentioned above, a matter of using the body in such a way that its natural balance is preserved and no unnecessary tension is set up. This is achieved in the first instance by directing the head forwards and upwards. The chin is kept parallel to the ground and the neck is allowed to move freely. The back is lengthened and broadened and the pelvis is tilted into its natural position by swinging the lower part forward. This avoids the hollow back or exaggerated 'lordosis' that produces lower back pain in many people. When sitting, the legs are not crossed and the feet placed firmly on the floor underneath the knees. When standing, the weight is distributed evenly over the soles of both feet. The shoulders are relaxed and the arms hang loosely by the sides.

Inhibiting   This means introducing a short pause between the decision to carry out an action and the action itself. This pause, which need only last a fraction of a second, gives one a chance to take charge of the action and to carry it out in a way which conforms to the principles of good use mentioned above. If this is not done, the chances are that the action will be carried out in an uncoordinated way and with an excessive expenditure of energy.

Inhibiting is also a way of increasing awareness and of living in the moment. Many people are so intent on achieving their next short-term aim that they are oblivious to the means whereby they achieve it. Their attention is always on some future goal and never on the path that leads to it. The end is always more important than the means. Yet it is the means whereby we achieve our aims which determine how we actually live. The quality of our lives depends on the present moment, not on some future event which may never happen. In fact it never does happen in a way which brings us satisfaction, because by that time our minds are fixed on something else. So inhibiting, even though the time involved is minimal, is a valuable addition to the quality of our movements and of our whole lives.

Directing   This means the conscious decision to move the body in a certain way. It follows immediately after inhibiting and is the execution of the decision to use the body in accordance with the principles of good use. In practice, directing usually means making a decision to let the head lead any movement and to direct it forwards and upwards. This is particularly important when changing from a sitting to a standing position or vice versa. The tendency is to allow the head to tilt backwards, and the decision to direct the head forwards and upwards counteracts this. It is also important when walking and, of course, when standing and speaking, as in the case of Alexander himself when he was an actor.

The Alexander Technique can be practised throughout the day by bringing awareness to every movement and to every posture adopted. There is, however, a particular exercise which is not only beneficial in re-educating the muscles in the principles of good use, but which is restful and energizing. It is the lying posture. It is carried out as follows.

Select several books with a total thickness of between 4–5 cm. Place them on the floor and sit down so that when you stretch out on your back the books will be under your head. Slowly bend backwards, allowing your spine to unroll, vertebra by vertebra, until you are lying horizontally, with the books under your head, supporting it.

Draw your feet back towards your buttocks and bend your knees. The knees should be close together but not touching. Rest your hands, palms downwards, on your stomach.

Check the angle of your chin. It should be in line with an imaginary vertical line to the ceiling. If your chin is tilted back from this line, your head is too far back and you should add another book to the pile. If your chin is forward of the vertical line, your head is too far forward and you have got too many books in the pile. Remove one and check the angle of the chin. If necessary keep on adjusting the number of books until you achieve the right angle for the chin. You will notice that, as you lie in this position, your pelvis is automatically tilted, so that the lower back part is rotated upwards. In a standing position this would mean that it would be rotated forwards, in accordance with the principles of good use mentioned above. So, lying in this position will give the body an opportunity of getting used to this posture. The position of the head, supported by the books, conforms to the 'forwards and upwards' principle mentioned and is a good preparation for standing and sitting.

Voice production

Standing in the correct Alexander position is the foundation of good voice production. As Alexander himself discovered, the quality of the voice depends on the position of the head and the ability of the larynx (the cavity which houses the vocal cords) and the vocal cords themselves to move freely. If the head is moved backwards the vocal cords are stretched and are unable to respond fully to the demands of voice production. If the head is in the forwards and upwards position the vocal cords are free to vibrate in a way which provides the voice with strength and resonance.

The next step in voice production is to become aware of the versatility of the voice and how this can be used to improve communication. A monotonous voice, which does not vary in pitch, volume or speed, is boring and will not be listened to with attention for long. A voice which is constantly varying these factors, and which is perhaps also coloured by musicality and emotion, will command attention. The content will be remembered. If a trainer wants to be listened to with attention, so that what she says is learned, she will pay attention to the way she uses her voice.

Each of the variants in voice production can be practised separately. Let us take pitch first. Pitch is the quality of sound governed by the rate of vibration of the vocal cords. If the cords vibrate at a high frequency, the pitch rises. If they vibrate at a low frequency, it falls. Few people make use of the full range of pitch of their voices. Try the following exercises to explore the range of pitch of your voice.

Exercise 1 (pitch) If possible, find a partner and stand opposite them, a few feet apart. Recite the alphabet, each person saying a letter in turn. Vary the pitch each time you say a letter. Work right through your range, from very low to very high and then change the pitch randomly. Do this several

Figure 11.1 *... a monotonous voice, which does not vary in pitch, volume or speed, is boring and will not be listened to with attention for long ...*

times, pushing your voice into higher and lower ranges of pitch and becoming aware of the sounds.

Exercise 2 (volume) Carry out the same exercise as above, but this time keep the pitch constant and vary the volume. Range from a whisper to a shout. Be aware of the power of the lower end of the range.

Exercise 3 Working with a partner again, each read from a book and sing the verbs. This introduces the concept of musicality into the voice. It may sound bizarre at first, but you should persevere until it feels natural and enjoyable.

Exercise 4 Engage in a standing 'conversation' with a partner, using the letters of the alphabet alone and introducing emotion through the use of intonation, that is, variations in the pitch and volume of your voice.

Exercise 5 Read passages from a book to a partner, consciously introducing as much variety of intonation and volume as possible. Try to make your voice interesting and compelling. Try memorizing short passages and give your partner eye contact as you are saying them.

Exercise 6 Stand about 20 paces away from a partner and read passages from a book to them. Stand in the Alexander position. Give eye contact.

Project your voice. Imagine that it is a jet of water and that you have to direct it precisely at the target. Imagine that you are addressing a large audience and that you are targeting your voice at different individuals in turn.

Exercise 7   Try singing a song when you are cleaning your teeth. The jaw will be open and be in the correct position for good voice production.

Exercise 8   Sing a song while towelling your back after a bath. Your awareness of your back will tend to make you produce the sound from this area.

Exercise 9   Read poetry or prose to a small audience. While doing so, be aware of the position of your body. Vary the pitch, volume and rhythm of your voice. Do not be afraid of exaggeration. Alternatively, make a recording of your voice while reading alone. Play it back and listen critically to the use you have made in the range of volume and pitch.

Notes and references

1 The Alexander Technique is usually taught on an individual basis and requires a minimum of about 25 hours of instruction from a trained teacher in order to master it. Such teachers are to be found in most parts of the UK. Their addresses can be supplied by the Society of Teachers of the Alexander Technique (see Appendix D for address).
For details of books on the Alexander Technique, refer to note 3 of Chapter 10.

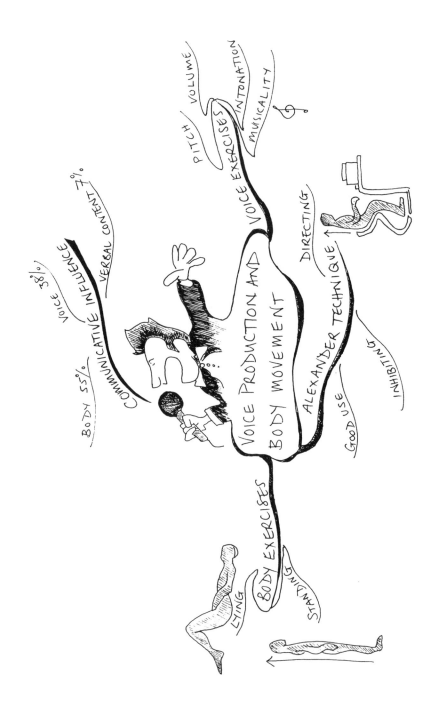

Mind map for Chapter 11—voice production and body movement

12 Inner awareness

Who looks outside, dreams;
who looks inside, wakes

C.G. Jung

Scene *The training room at Glospot Ltd. Warren Bird, the marketing director, could not understand why his lesson on product policy was not going well. He had prepared it in great detail and had produced a considerable number of OHP slides. The lesson covered the overall product objective, the product analysis sheet and the marketing audit. He had assembled all the relevant facts and his slides were clear and attractively designed.*

But the group of seven salespeople were undoubtedly bored. Furthermore, they seemed depressed and lacking in energy. There was an air of listlessness and they were clearly not learning.

Afterwards Warren decided to ask David Copeland, the sales manager, why he thought the lesson had not been a success.

'Well, since you ask me,' he replied, 'there were three reasons, at least as far as I'm concerned. The first was this letter we'd all received from your brother, Jack. Didn't you know about it? It said that complaints had been received from the production staff about the salesforce. Apparently they were not supplying accurate information about the glazes required by our contract customers. It was the way he put it. Really got our backs up.

Secondly, you looked when you came in as if you'd just had an almighty row with someone and were about to take it out on us. The way you stormed into the room and slammed your pile of slides down on the table! And the way you dealt with questions seemed to confirm that you were angry about something. It was a real turn-off.

Another thing—you never gave us any chance to move or talk to anyone else. We just sat there and listened to you. To be frank, it was dead boring.'

Warren thought about these remarks and started to take stock of himself. It became clear to him that, although he had spent a lot of time preparing the content of his lesson, he had spent none at all in considering its subconscious aspects. He had, in fact, had a flaming row that morning. It had been with his brother, Jack, about the letter which he had sent to the sales staff without consulting him. It had been exacerbated by a previous disagreement they had had over company training policy. It had got out of hand and Warren had lost his temper. He had obviously carried his anger with him into the classroom.

He realized, too, that he had failed to pick up the signals of depression in the group and to make allowances for their mood. If he had aired the subject uppermost in their minds and given them an opportunity of expressing their feelings, he might have then gained their attention.

On further reflection he became aware that his lesson had failed to involve the group actively. He remembered that there were several members who were constantly fidgeting and clearly wanting to move.

He wondered, too, if he could have done something to bring in some kind of human interest in his talk. Perhaps he had concentrated too much on facts and figures. Could this have contributed to the boredom which was so clearly evident?

The fact is, that no matter how well we as trainers prepare our lessons, if we neglect the subconscious aspects at work in the classroom, our lessons will not be successful. If we want them to succeed, we must take the time to become aware, at an inner level, of ourselves and of the people we are teaching.

Physical and emotional state

The first aspect of this inner awareness is our physical and emotional state. It is only too easy to go into a classroom carrying with us negative emotions. These will transmit themselves very quickly to the members of the group. Over 90 per cent of what we communicate in a classroom is non-verbal (see Chapter 11). Our trainees pick up our mood very quickly from the way we hold ourselves, our facial expression and our tone of voice. We are in a position of great influence when we are in charge of a group under training. Our mood, whether it be good or bad, will soon be reflected in the individuals who make up the class.

So what can we do about it? We all have periods of anxiety, anger and depression. Do our classes have to share them with us and thus learn less well than they could do? No, because we can to a large extent take charge of our moods and our emotions. We can do so because of a simple fact; one which not many people are aware of on a practical level. The link between our bodies and our minds is two-way. When we feel depressed our mood is reflected in our body and our voice. Our head hangs forward, our shoulders droop and our facial expression takes on an air of gloom. Our eyes fail to make contact with others. Our voice becomes low-pitched and monotonous. There is no mistaking the signals. Conversely, when we feel happy and optimistic, we tend to stand tall, to smile, to look the world in the face and to talk in a lively manner.

In both these cases the body is reflecting the emotion which is uppermost in our mind. But we can reverse the process. By acting as if we feel good we can actually make ourselves have that feeling. So even if we start the day feeling pessimistic and ill-tempered, we can make our body and voice behave as if we feel optimistic and cheerful. We can stand up straight, breathe deeply, smile, move vigorously and modulate the pitch and volume of our voice. We can create in our mind a picture of ourselves vibrant with energy and enthusiasm. In a short while we will find that our feelings are changing. We feel better. We feel, in fact, as we would if our emotional state were such as to generate the behaviour we have deliberately created. We have taken charge of our emotions.

So, what we must do is to stop and take stock of ourselves before we go into a classroom. If our emotional state is not appropriate, we must take the necessary steps to change it. There are a number of ways in which we can do this. They are described in the chapters on the Body mind link (Chapter 9), Voice production and body movement (Chapter 11) and Visualization (Chapter 13).

Brain function

Let us now look at another aspect of inner awareness—the way in which our brain functions. We have seen in Chapter 8 how we can become aware of the different learning styles of the members of a group, and make allowances for our own preferred style of thinking. These thinking and learning styles are based on the concept of brain dominance.

Establishing our own brain dominance and constantly making allowances for it is an essential part of inner awareness. So the first step is to have our brain dominance assessed. We can do this with the Herrmann Brain Dominance Instrument, the Brain Map or one of the other tests described in Chapter 8. When we plan our lessons we should always have our brain-dominance profile in mind. We should be aware that every teaching point needs to be put across not just in a way which suits our own brain preference, but in a way which makes it easy for people of different brain dominances to learn.

So if, for instance, we are teaching about marketing audits and we know that our dominance is in the top left quadrant of the HBDI, we will not be content with just showing graphs and giving out factual information. We will think of ways of appealing to people who want some emotional or inter-personal aspect of the subject (bottom right quadrant), or who want an overview of it and some idea of how it might contribute to the achievement of long-term aims (top right quadrant). We will then give some thought to our preferred sensory modality—in other words, whether our natural preference is to convey the information by means of visual aids, by talking or by some kind of physical activity. Again, we will look at each teaching point and make sure that we plan to present it in a way which appeals to all three kinds of learner.

In both cases we can use visualization to plan the conduct of the lesson. We can relax, close our eyes and create a mental film of the conduct of the lesson, seeing clearly the ways in which we involve people of different learning styles.

The next step in inner awareness is to pause and take stock of our own emotional state. If we have just had a row with a colleague we can become aware of our anger and make a conscious decision to change this inappropriate emotion, before we go into our classroom. We can carry out some of the exercises at our disposal to change our emotional state.

We might release the anger by shouting and breaking an imaginary stick across our knees. We might tense and relax our muscles. We might do some deep abdominal breathing. We might spend a few minutes in a chair relaxing and creating mental images of a peaceful scene. We might walk in a calm and poised manner, acting as if this were our mental state. There are many ways in which we can change our emotional state, but we might only have time for one and this might be enough.

The above are measures which we can take immediately before entering our classroom. Once in the classroom, we can use our powers of observation to become aware of the emotional and physical state of the members of the group. Body language and facial expression will tell us a great deal. If people are sitting slumped and listless we can assume that the energy level is low, possibly because of a prolonged session sitting without movement in a poorly ventilated room or for some other reason. We can take steps to raise energy. For instance we can open the windows to allow fresh air into the room. We can do some energy-raising exercises, such as the cross crawl or we can start with a group activity (see Chapter 9, Energy).

If we notice that people are looking depressed or angry we can ask questions until we find out the reason. If it is something like a letter from the company affecting their remuneration or giving them warning of impending redundancies, we can show our understanding by allowing a few minutes for people to talk about the problem. This establishes rapport and demonstrates to the group that we understand and are sympathetic. The very fact of expressing in words the thoughts that are worrying them may have the effect of releasing the negative emotion. Once expressed openly a worrying thought often loses its power.

Throughout the lesson we need to be aware of the participation level of each individual. A person who withdraws eye contact and shows by their body language that they have lost interest, may well be having problems in understanding or may have raised an unconscious logical or emotional barrier. If we are aware of this we can try to find out the reason for the behaviour and help the individual to continue to learn. Ignoring the behaviour may mean a wasted lesson for the person concerned.

So, inner awareness is an important element in becoming a creative trainer. As Dag Hammarskold said: 'The more faithfully you listen to the voice within you, the better you will hear what is sounding outside.'

Notes

The following are some books which may help you to develop inner awareness:

Ferrucci, P. (1982) *What we may be—The visions and techniques of psychosynthesis*, Turnstone Press, Wellingborough, Northants.

Glouberman, D. (1989) *Life choices and life changes through imagework*, Unwin Hyman Ltd., London.

Lazarus, A. (1984) *In the mind's eye—The power of imagery for personal enrichment*, The Guildford Press, NY USA.

Robbins, A. (1986) *Unlimited power*, Simon & Schuster, London.

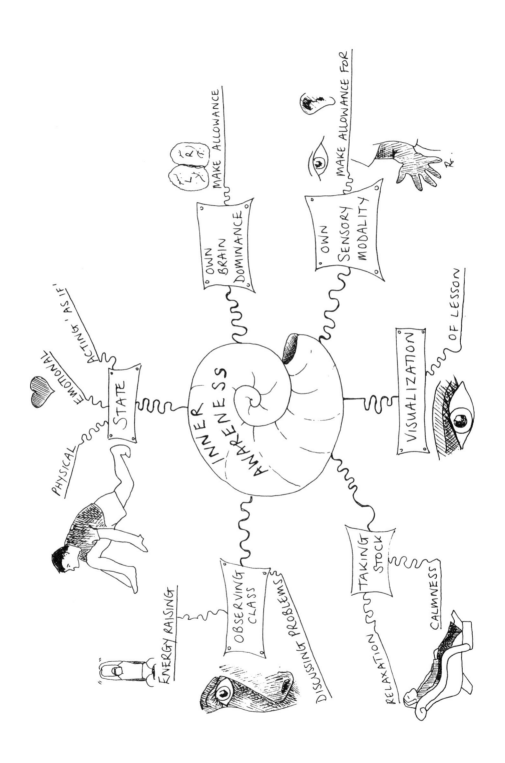

Mind map for Chapter 12—inner awareness

13 Visualization

Scene *The Glospot boardroom. The table was pushed back and a group of eleven directors and managers were sitting in a semi-circle.*

'*I've asked you all to come to this session with Tony,' said Jill Bird, looking around the group, 'because I think our company needs a clearer idea of where it's going. We've been doing more or less the same thing now for 23 years— ever since I took over from my father-in-law, in fact. But the world is changing around us. New technologies are being introduced in both glazing and firing. The European Union means that competition is growing. Our customers' tastes are changing. It's no wonder that our sales have remained more or less static for the past seven years. It seems to me that we need a clearer idea of where we are going—a vision of the future. As some of you know, I'm thinking of taking a less active role in the company soon. So it's really your vision, not mine, that's important. So I've asked Tony to facilitate a session on creating a joint vision for the company. Over to you, Tony.'*

Eleven pairs of eyes turned expectantly towards Tony Wakeman, who was sitting at the other end of the semi-circle of chairs, awaiting his cue. He stood up and moved deliberately into the open space at the end of the semi-circle. He smiled and looked round the group. He noticed that several members were sitting with crossed arms and legs, with expressions that were clearly sceptical.

'*Good morning, everyone,' began Tony. 'I can understand that some of you may be a bit suspicious of the word "vision". But, if you think about it, we're all creating visions of the future the whole time. Half of you, I imagine, are at this moment thinking not of what I'm saying, but of what you are planning to do in your office when you get back there. In other words, you are visualizing the future. There is nothing mysterious about it. It's just a question of becoming conscious of the process and using it for a specific purpose. You can learn to do this by using techniques based on our knowledge of how the brain works.'*

'Why don't we just get on with it and say where we think the company should be going?' said Jack Bird. 'I've got quite a few ideas.'

'We could do that, of course,' replied Tony. 'But we might be excluding some interesting alternatives. Anyway, let's try it. I'd like to start with some relaxation exercises. Then I'm going to ask you to spend a few minutes focusing your attention on your breath. After that I'm going to invite you to start allowing your thoughts to create pictures of possible futures for the company. Try to make these pictures multi-sensory. In other words, hear sounds. Try stepping into the pictures and getting a feeling for what it might be like to be there physically. After that you'll need one of these large sheets of paper and some coloured pens, which I'm going to give you now. You'll be making mind maps.'

Visualization is a highly effective and much neglected aspect of training. It can be used in many ways, of which the following are perhaps the most relevant:

1 To create a clear mental picture of a personal or organizational goal
2 To arouse interest in a new subject and awaken a desire to acquire more knowledge about it
3 To assist understanding of a technical process
4 To clarify learning and achievement goals and to strengthen belief in the ability to achieve them
5 To improve commitment to carrying out a plan
6 To provide a stimulus for creative thinking
7 To enhance self-image as a learner and achiever

Before looking at each of these in turn we should distinguish between guided and self-directed visualization (see the section 'Applications of visualization later in this chapter). In the former, the course tutor guides the members of the group by using words to suggest images in their minds. In the latter, the individuals of the group are given some general guidelines and produce their own mental images.

To be effective, visualization should not be restricted to visual images. It should bring in the other senses as well. These should include hearing (auditory) and physical movement and feeling (kinesthetic). They might sometimes include taste and smell. Most people find it easier to create images in one sense more than the others. For the majority it is the visual sense which is easiest and strongest, but others find it easier to create mental sounds or the feeling of physical movement or touch.

If you are guiding a group in a visualization it is therefore important to bring in as many senses as possible. Encourage the listeners to hear sounds, experience muscle movements and be aware of touch and feelings. If you are directing yourself, make a deliberate effort to bring in all the senses, not just the ones you find easiest to evoke.

The reason for bringing in all the senses in this way is that the subconscious mind will react to a clear, multi-sensory mental image as if it were reality. It has no means of distinguishing between this and the real thing.

Most people are good at producing realistic negative images, even if they are not aware that they are doing so. The person who is afraid of flying is producing highly convincing multi-sensory images of disasters—fire, explosion, panic and death. And because the subconscious mind takes them to be real it sends out signals which modify the person's behaviour accordingly. He or she will avoid flying whenever possible. If they have to fly they will exhibit all the symptoms—sweaty palms, increased rate of heart beat, dry throat—of someone in a real aircraft emergency.

Managers do exactly the same thing when they think negatively about the future. The sales manager sees sales dropping or failing to meet the target. The production manager sees output falling or held up due to strike action. The personnel manager sees key staff shortages. The managing director sees a hostile takeover bid. They react in the same way as the fearful air traveller—and they exhibit the same symptoms. These are the classic symptoms of stress and they frequently lead to a falling off in performance or ill health or both.

By taking charge of this unconscious mental process it is possible to turn it to one's advantage. The air traveller can create a picture in his or her mind of a peaceful, enjoyable flight and a safe arrival. The manager can see sales increasing, production flowing as planned, key staff recruited easily and a takeover bid successfully resisted. The subconscious mind will accept these messages as valid and produce actions which will tend to make them become reality.

Some people, however, find it quite difficult to take charge of the creation of mental images and they may need to learn techniques which will help them to do so. In fact, everyone can benefit from doing some preliminary exercises before starting to visualize. The key elements are relaxation, concentration and mind calming. They are described in Chapter 9. The following are some suggested guidelines for using them with the specific aim of preparing for visualization.

Preparing for visualization

1 Sit in an upright, relaxed position. Lying down or leaning back in a comfortable armchair will make it easier to relax, and if this is the only aim, this is fine. However, in order to visualize successfully it is necessary to remain alert. The best way of doing this is to keep the spine straight.

Start by asking the group to stretch their arms above their heads, take a deep breath and then lean slowly forward, breathing out and dropping their arms and heads down between their knees. When they sit up they should keep their backs straight and their legs uncrossed and rest their palms on their knees. This is sometimes known as the Pharaoh position and this is a good model to keep in mind.

2 Carry out some relaxation exercises, as described in Chapter 9. For instance, tense and relax the hands, arms, feet, legs, stomach and face, or imagine that the limbs are becoming progressively heavy and warm.

3 Breathe deeply several times.

4 Focus the attention on something which will prevent the mind from wandering. The object of concentration can be the breath, a sound or a visual image, such as a picture or a candle flame.

5 Create a mental picture of a place where the individual feels safe and peaceful. This could be on a beach by the sea, beside a lake, in a forest or on a mountain. Give a certain amount of preliminary guidance and then let the members of the group fill in the details.

Here are some general guidelines to follow when visualizing or guiding others to visualize. Following them will make the mental images clearer and more credible to the subconscious mind:

- **Involve as many of the senses as possible.** Seeing, hearing, touching, tasting and smelling. Use movement, too, if possible.
- **Ask the participants to describe to a partner the mental images they are seeing.** This activates the left brain as well as the right and adds considerably to the effect on the speaker.
- **Add as many details as possible and avoid vague concepts.** Include colours, contrast, depth and movement.
- **Transform abstract ideas into concrete examples or symbols.** For example, instead of the general idea of 'success', see a detailed picture of the moment when success is achieved—in full multi-sensory detail.
- **Include emotions, when appropriate.** Help individuals to feel excitement, a sense of achievement, pride, etc.
- **Be patient.** Do not expect immediate results. The subconscious mind has had years to acquire the habit of negative image forming. It may take some weeks or months of regular practise to change the habit. Encourage course participants to practise regularly on their own—at least twice a day. This can be done in bed prior to going to sleep at night or on waking in the morning.
- **If appropriate, add affirmations to the mental images.** These should be short, strong and positive. They are powerful additional agents for change. Examples are: 'I am a capable and efficient manager (supervisor, computer programmer, etc.)', 'I am a dedicated and successful learner', 'I am creative and visionary in my life and in my work'.

- **Consider the use of music**. Baroque music or certain types of New Age music make a very effective background to your voice and appeal to the right brain (see Chapter 4, Music).

Applications of visualization

Let us now look at the applications of visualization mentioned at the beginning of this chapter.

Arousing interest in a new subject

The brain's limbic system filters all incoming information. It only allows information to go straight in to the long-term memory if it has some emotional content. It is important, therefore, to create at the outset a link between the new subject and some form of pleasant emotion. One way to do this is by guided visualization.

Let us take as an example a lesson to the staff of the accounting department on the subject of dealing with the financing of export orders. Glospot has recently had an order from Russia, so let us take this country as an example.

Ask the participants to do some stretching, breathing and relaxation exercises (see above and Chapter 9). Then, in a quiet voice, with frequent pauses and possibly a musical background, you might say something like this:

> 'Close your eyes. Imagine that you are in Moscow. It is snowing and you are walking down Gorky Street. In spite of your warm fur coat and hat you can feel the bitter cold of the Russian winter. You hear the sound of Russian voices from passers-by and you see around you crowds of people in great-coats and mufflers hurrying home. You come to an enormous building with the words GYM written over it and you go in. It is a department store—the biggest you have ever seen. It is warm and there is Russian folk music playing. On the shelves are attractive examples of Russian handicraft—tunics, blankets, dolls, pottery, etc. You ask for assistance from one of the dark-haired sales women and she replies in good English and with a smile. A shopper next to you hears that you are a foreigner and joins in the con-versation. Others join in, too, and you enjoy your first real contact with Russian people. You are invited to have a glass of vodka in a neighbouring bar. You return to your hotel that evening with a warm feeling about Mos-cow and the Russian people.'

You then ask the participants to imagine that they have been invited to sit in on an interview between a Russian bank manager and a representative from their own company. The bank manager tells the representative how to go about arranging a letter of credit to finance the order.

Assisting understanding of a technical process

Visualization can be a very effective way of helping trainees to understand an unfamiliar and complicated technical process. The memorization and understanding of formulae is one area where it can be particularly useful. Let us take as an example a formula from the world of petroleum companies. It is a formula used to assess the rate of fluid flow of oil in a porous medium. It is called Darcy's Law:

$$q = \frac{Q}{A} = -K \cdot \frac{1}{\mu} \cdot \left(\frac{P\text{-}P}{L}\right)$$

Where Q   = fluid flow rate (cc/sec)
         A   = cross section area (cm)
         μ = fluid viscosity (cp)
         L   = length (cm)
         P-P   = pressure difference (atm)
         K   = permeability of media (Darcy's)

The group members are asked to lie on their backs and, after some relaxation exercises, to imagine that they are a layer of underground porous sand, through which oil is passing. They feel the rate of flow increasing as the pressure difference builds up and the viscosity of the oil decreases. Another example is the operation of an electronic micro switch. Participants are invited to imagine that they are an electron flowing along the circuit.

Clarifying learning and achievement goals

You can use visualization to help members of the group to establish a clear goal. By examining on a mental screen various scenarios and their consequences, the trainees can gradually become clear in their minds about what they really want. Having done this, they should make a commitment towards achieving the goal, perhaps writing it down, setting deadlines and drawing up a plan.

Strengthening belief and motivation

When the goal is quite clear, the outcome, with all its advantageous consequences, is visualized in full multi-sensory detail. If it is described to a partner the effect is increased considerably. The goal becomes almost a tangible reality. The subconscious mind accepts it as such and works towards its fulfilment. If the visualization is practised regularly by the individual it is highly motivating.

Stimulus for creative thinking

You can help a group to come up with creative ideas for the benefit of their company or to solve problems by encouraging them to use visualization. Before doing this, however, a good deal of logical and analytical preparatory work may need to be done. The facts must be established and the desired outcome clearly stated. It may be advantageous to have a discussion or brain storming session in advance in order to get the thinking process started. Then the group members can be invited to relax, clear their minds and allow thoughts related to the problem to float into their minds in the form of visual images. They should have a pencil and paper beside them so as to be able to make notes if necessary. Talking about their ideas to a partner may help individuals to clarify them. Later the ideas can be aired in a group discussion. A cooperative group, operating with the ground rule of no criticism at this stage, may well take a half-formed, impractical idea and transform it into one with real potential.

Enhancing self-image as a learner and/or achiever

A surprising number of people, even those in positions of authority and those with impressive academic achievements, have a poor image of themselves in their subconscious minds. This usually goes back to childhood, when they were led to believe by their parents or teachers that they were not good at a particular subject or even generally useless. This image may be very firmly rooted and may be an obstacle to the realization of potential, either in their jobs or in their learning ambitions.

This negative image can be replaced by a positive one through guided, and later through self-directed, visualization. It can be achieved by asking the members of the group, after they have carried out the relaxation exercises, to recall a successful experience in their earlier lives. This experience should, if possible, be similar to the one which they are currently finding difficult.

For example, if someone is convinced that they cannot learn a foreign language, they might recall an incident at school when they received praise from their teacher for doing particularly well in an English, history or geography test. If this is not possible, then they might recall success in a science subject or even in a sport, such as football. They recall a particular incident related to the success and describe it to a partner, getting in touch with the feeling they experienced at that time.

While they are experiencing the feeling, they touch a point on their left

Figure 13.1 ... *a surprising number of people have a poor image of themselves in their subconscious minds. This usually goes back to their childhood ...*

hand or wrist with their right forefinger and thumb. This is called 'anchoring' and the technique is taken from Neuro-Linguistic Programming.[1] It creates a link between the physical action and the neurological pathways of the brain which are responsible for generating the feeling experienced during the successful achievement. Once the anchor has been established by practice, the person imagines stepping into a future situation when they need to speak a foreign language and activating ('firing') the anchor. The same feeling of confidence will return. This technique requires practice, but it is remarkably effective in overcoming learning blocks and lack of confidence.

Rehearsing a physical skill

The neural pathways in the brain, which are activated when a person creates a clear mental image of performing an action, are similar to the ones used when they actually perform the action. So a new skill can be rehearsed by visualizing oneself doing it, particularly if the kinesthetic sense is involved. This concept was used by Timothy Gallwey in his best-selling book *The Inner Game of Tennis*[2] and in the many other books on sport written subsequently featuring visualization.

The same idea can be used to learn skills in industry or commerce, such as throwing a pot or operating a word processor.

The above examples are only some of the ways in which you as a trainer and as an individual can use visualization to enhance the quality of your work and of your life. Other areas in which it can be employed with great effect are:

- **Memory**. Names, statistics, facts, lists, etc.[3]
- **Positive attitude**. Individuals, and sometimes whole management teams, can sometimes become victims of negative thought patterns. This is particularly true in industries which are declining or where the market conditions are adverse. These negative attitudes can be transformed by deliberately generating mental images of successful outcomes, perhaps in different fields.
- **Forecasting**. Accurate and reliable forecasting is a priceless asset to any company. Visualization can be used to enhance its accuracy and to anticipate problems before they occur.
- **Ethical values**. Some companies are guilty of ecological damage and others of manufacturing products which have detrimental effects on people. The executives in the companies who are responsible do not act out of any evil intent. They are simply unaware, or unwilling to become aware, of the consequences of what they are doing. Guided visualization can be used to help them achieve this awareness and may lead to steps being taken which mitigate the harmful consequences of the company's activities.
  An increasing number of companies are becoming more 'green' in their approach and this often has a positive effect on their public image and their balance sheet. The training officer can help the employees of the company to undergo the mental transformation

which will make their company's commitment to ethical values a lasting one (see Chapter 7).[4]

Notes and references

1   See, O'Connor, J. and Seymour, J. (1993) *Introducing Neuro-Linguistic Programming* (p. 56), Aquarian Press, Wellingborough.
2   Gallwey, T. (1974) *The Inner Game of Tennis*, Bantam Books, London.
3   See, Buzan, T. (1988) *Make the Most of your Mind*, Pan Books, London and Lawlor, M. (1988) *Inner Track Learning*, Pilgrims Publications, Kemble. The latter is available from Forge House Centre; see Appendix D for address.
4   Some of the many books on the subject of visualization are:
    Maltz, M. (1960) *Psycho-cybernetics*, Prentice Hall, Englewood Cliffs, New Jersey USA.
    Odle, C. (1990) *Practical Visualization*, Aquarian Press, Wellingborough.
    Page, M. (1990) *Visualization—The key to fulfilment*, Aquarian Press, Wellingborough.
    Shone, R. (1984) *Creative Visualization*, Thorsons Publishing Group, Wellingborough, Northants.
    Sommer, R. (1978) *The Mind's Eye—Imagery in Everyday Life*, Delta Publishing, New York USA.
    Syer, J. and Connolly, C. (1991) *Think to Win*, Simon & Schuster, London.

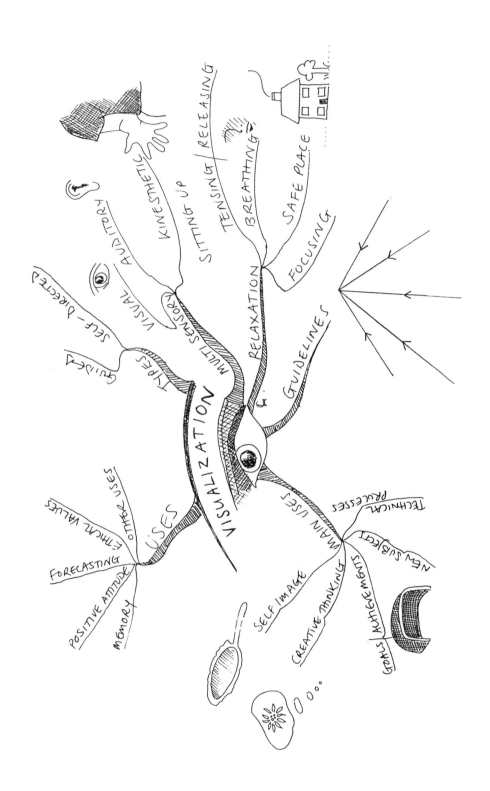

Mind map for Chapter 13—visualization

PART 4

The learner's perspective

14 Study skills 1

*They know enough who know how
to learn*

Henry Adams

Scene *The training room at Glospot Ltd.*

'Good morning,' said Tony Wakeman, as he entered the training room and saw in front of him the 12 expectant faces of the moulding shop trainees. 'I understand that each one of you is determined to get an NVQ in forming ceramic items. Right?'

Twelve heads nodded in agreement.

'Okay. Now if I understand the situation correctly, you are going to have to work on your own a good deal. So you will need to know how to go about learning. What I'm going to give you today is a model which you can use to learn anything. Does that sound interesting?'

There was a murmur of agreement. Then, after getting them into groups to discuss how they went about learning at the moment, Tony proceeded to give them a puppet play. There were murmurs of surprise and a few giggles as Tony reached into his capacious briefcase and took out two glove puppets. One was a young man with a smock and a head of tousled flaxen hair and the other a young, dark-haired woman, with eyes like saucers. The following dialogue took place between the puppets, called Paul and Maria.

Maria: Hello Paul. You look rather depressed. What's the matter?

Paul: I'm fed up Maria. I can't seem to get anywhere with studying for my NVQ.

Maria: Perhaps I can help you, Paul. I've just passed mine. Like you, I felt really low and thought I could never learn all that stuff. Then I discovered something called Accelerated Learning. It made a big difference.

Paul: Tell me about it, Maria.

Maria: Well, first you must find out what kind of a learner you are and make sure you get the facts in a way which suits your own learning style. Then you

The creative trainer

need to realize that there are three stages to learning anything. The first is what you do beforehand. The second is what you do during and the third is what you do after learning.

Paul: Oh? I just open my book and get down to studying.

Maria: That won't get you very far, Paul. First of all you need to get your environment right. You need to associate learning with enjoyment, not pain. And you actually retain things better when you're relaxed.

Paul: I thought learning was hard work, Maria. That's what I've always been told.

Maria: Yes, and that's why you avoid it whenever you can, Paul. You've got to change your attitude. Then you need to relax and picture some of your past successes and remind yourself that you are able to learn. Then see yourself having successfully completed the course. Not only see it, but hear it and feel it—as if you were really there in the future.

Your responsibility as a trainer should not end when your course participants leave the classroom. If you want them to retain the information and use it actively, you may have to give them some advice about learning to learn. The following are some suggestions.

Determining individual learning styles

You can help your course participants to learn better by making them aware of how their individual brains prefer to receive and process the information which you are giving them. As outlined in Chapter 8, there are two aspects of the brain which need to be considered: brain dominance which can be established in the way described in Chapter 8 and preferred sensory modality. Again, refer to Chapter 8 for guidance on how to establish whether a learner is visual, auditory or kinesthetic.

You can help learners to gain more from their periods of individual study by recognizing these natural preferences and adapting their learning activities accordingly.

Before the study session

Getting into the right frame of mind

A surprising number of people have a negative image of themselves as learners. This applies particularly to older people, who may fear that their age may be a handicap. Many younger people have memories of unsuccessful experiences at school and may lack confidence. Lack of motivation is another problem. Furthermore, relatively few people have a clear picture of their learning goal. All of these potential obstacles need to be addressed if learning is to be successful.

To be successful in the long term, the learner needs to have a strong desire to master the subject. This means engaging the emotions or the affective part of the brain. This is located, as we have seen in Chapter 8, in the limbic system. To use computer terminology, it is a matter of programming the mind so that the emotions are engaged in a positive and not a negative way. We might call this 'Affective Programming'. This is carried out by visualization, in a state of physical relaxation. Although it takes some time to describe the process on paper, with practise it need only take a few minutes.

To start with the learner should carry out one or more of the relaxation exercises described in Chapter 9. Then he or she should carry out some or all of the following affective programming visualizations.

Accessing a resourceful state[1]

Recall a time when you have just done something successfully. This could be something you have learned in a formal setting, such as a laboratory experiment or writing a difficult essay. It could also be something you have done in your non-academic life, like scoring a goal in a football match or playing a guitar for the first time in a gig. See it from the outside, with yourself in the scene, as if you were an observer. Then step into your body and experience it in full multi-sensory detail. See colours, details and movement. Listen to sounds. Feel physical sensations. Experience the particular emotion or feeling you felt at that time. When the feeling is at its height, press your forefinger and thumb lightly onto your right wrist (or other part of your body) and hold it there for a short time (about half a minute is usually enough). This process will 'anchor' the physical action to the emotional state. In future, if you wish to recall the feeling of success, all you need to do is to repeat the pressure on the same spot. It may also be helpful, while doing this, to repeat a short sentence (an 'affirmation'), confirming your belief in yourself as a successful learner.

Goal visualization

Create a mental picture of yourself at a time and in a particular place where you are experiencing the benefits of the study you are now undertaking. Again, see it first from the outside and then step into your body. See and feel it in multi-sensory detail. Make an affirmation about achieving the goal which will result in your being in this situation.

Stages of learning

Visualize the exact place or places in which you will be carrying out your study. See yourself first from the outside and then imagine yourself in your body. Make the place as pleasant as possible, bringing in any sounds, such as your favourite music, smells, maybe of fresh flowers, and visual elements, such as colours, interesting wall posters and mobiles. Get a feeling of the excitement you are experiencing by acquiring the new knowledge. Look at a clock and note the time. Look at a wall calendar and note the day of the week and the month. Be aware that this is part of a carefully structured plan, each study session bringing you nearer to your goal.

Learning blocks[2]   If you suffer from one of the learning blocks mentioned above (negative memories from school, fear that you are too old, etc.) you may wish to try the following visualization.

Create in your mind a picture of yourself going through the worst situation that you can recall or imagine, past or future, connected with your learning. See it as clearly as you can from the point of view of an outside observer. Play through the action as if you were watching a video recording of it. Play it through again, this time with the action speeded up, as if you were operating the fast forward button. Now rewind it and see it played backwards. Now see it without colour, as if watching it on an old black and white television set. Now see it getting further away, as if it were fading into the distance.

Now imagine playing a new video cassette. This one is of yourself in a completely successful learning situation. Adjust the colours to make them as brilliant as possible. Turn up the sound. Add music. Zoom in for a close-up of yourself. Now step into your body and experience the situation with all your senses, especially the kinesthetic. Feel what it is like. Now step out again and run the film through once more, adding any details which make it more attractive. Realize that you have a choice as to which of the two scenes you are going to make your reality.

Harmonizing the   If you are going to get the most out of your brain during your study
mind and the body   session, it is important that you take your body into consideration. Your energy level should be right for the task in hand and your brain should have enough oxygen to function efficiently.

The first thing to do is to assess your energy level. You may find it useful to use the Energy Chart shown in Appendix C. If you fill this in systematically every hour or so for two days, you will achieve a level of awareness of your energy which will stay with you. This will enable you to take whatever action is necessary to correct it.

The most likely realization that you will come to is that your energy level is too low, particularly if you are studying in the evening after a day's work or when you are tired after some physical activity. The most useful form of exercise you can take in this situation is some of the Brain Gym exercises. These not only raise energy, but help to connect up the parts of the brain needed for particular study activities, such as reading, creative thinking, maths or writing. See Chapter 9 for a description of some of these exercises.

Alternatively, if your body feels stiff and you are lacking oxygen, you can carry out some of the Office Yoga exercises also described in Chapter 9.

Asking 'What's in it   It may be useful to take a piece of paper and a pencil and to note down
for me?'   the precise benefits which you will get from acquiring the knowledge

contained in this study session. These may be related to an exam or to your working or private life. Being clear about these benefits will help to motivate you.

The 'during' and 'after' stages of learning are covered in the next chapter.[3]

Notes and references

1 O'Connor, J. and Seymour, J. (1993) *Introducing Neuro-Linguistic Programming* (pp. 54–59), Aquarian Press, Wellingborough.
2 Bandler, R. (1985) *Using Your Brain—For a Change—Neuro-Linguistic Programming* (pp. 98–100), Real People Press, Moab, Utah USA.
3 All three stages are described in greater detail in Lawlor, M. (1988) *Inner Track Learning*, Pilgrims Publications, Kemble.

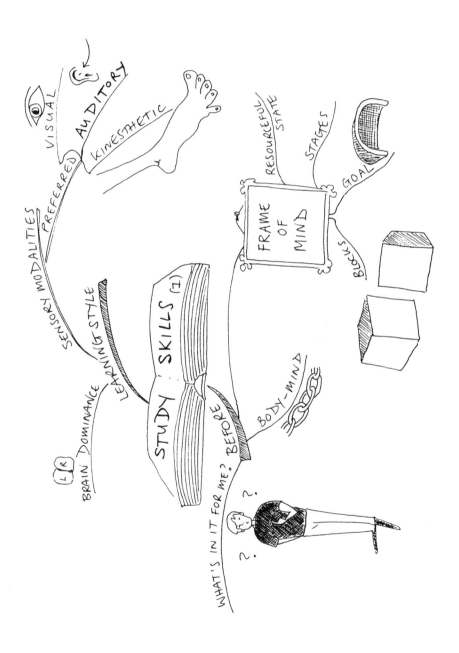

Mind map for Chapter 14—study skills (1)

15 Study skills 2

*We possess only that which we
have conquered for ourselves*

Jean Piaget

Scene *The Glospot training room. The NVQ class had reassembled for their
second session on learning to learn and Tony started the session with some
'connecting' games and a Brain Gym exercise designed to stimulate memory.
He then used a koosh ball to elicit from the group, standing in a circle, the
main points about learning from the puppet play in the previous lesson. He
then resumed the puppet play (see Chapter 14 for the first act).*

*Paul: Hello there, Maria. It's great to see you. I've been trying out some of
those visualization exercises you gave me and they worked a treat.*

*Maria: That's great, Paul. But that was only the beginning. Now comes the
second stage, which is actually learning about the subject. What you need to
be now is an active, not a passive, learner. First draw up a list of questions
about what you are learning. Don't take anything for granted. And you need
to use all of your intelligences.*

Paul: All my intelligences?

*Maria: Yes. Didn't you know that you have seven intelligences? Some are
more highly developed in each of us than others. But we can make use of them
all in learning.*

Paul: I thought people were either intelligent or not.

*Maria: I haven't got time to go into it now, Paul, but I'll make out a list of
the seven intelligences for you and also let you have some tips about finding
out which are your strong and weak ones. The next thing you have to do is to
memorize the key points about the thing you're studying.*

*Paul: Ah, that's where the problem lies, Maria. I can't remember new things
at all. My teacher told me at school that I had a terrible memory.*

*Maria: And you believed it, I suppose. Well, Paul, there are lots of memory
techniques which you can use and which will give you a near perfect memory.
Making mind maps is one. Mnemonics is another. But again, I haven't got*

time to tell you about them now. A few more tips about what to do when you're learning: Take plenty of short breaks—at least every 40 minutes. And keep your energy level up. Do some Brain Gym exercises. These help to keep your brain connected up for learning. Drink plenty of water. And sit up with a straight back. Don't lean back in a comfortable chair or you'll lose concentration.

Paul: I hope I can remember all this, Maria. You said something, too, about what to do after the learning session. What's that?

Maria: Revision, Paul. It's very important. Otherwise you'll forget half of what you've learned within 24 hours. But you need to do it in an active way. Re-draw your mind maps. Test yourself with flash cards. Write about the subject in a journal. Talk about it with a circle of friends who are studying the same thing. Find someone to teach it to. And reactivate the knowledge regularly until you're certain it's in your long-term memory.

This chapter follows on directly from Chapter 14, from preparing for the study session.

During the study session

Having prepared yourself physically and mentally, you can now begin the actual study session. The guiding principle is to be pro-active and not passive. In other words, take charge of your learning.

Your learning style

Decide, in the light of the assessment of your brain dominance and your preferred sensory modalities, how you are going to go about the learning task. Are you going to read (if you are a visual learner), listen to a tape or perhaps read aloud dramatically (if you are an auditory learner), or become involved in some physical activity such as role playing or mind mapping (if you are a kinesthetic learner)? Are you going to apply analysis and logic (if you are a quadrant A thinker), are you going to organize and plan your study sequentially (if you are a quadrant B thinker), are you going to share ideas with others and perhaps bring in some emotional involvement (if you are a quadrant C thinker) or are you going to explore hidden possibilities and construct concepts (if you are a quadrant D thinker)? (See Chapter 8.)

Ask questions

Draw up a list of questions concerning the subject you are about to study. Do not accept blindly what you read or hear. Constantly ask yourself whether the new information fits in with your present understanding and whether it can be accepted as being applicable to your situation. Try to create as many associations as possible between the new information and your existing knowledge of the subject.

Get an overview

Always start any study session with an overview of what you are about to learn. If it is a book, skim through it, looking at chapter and paragraph headings and possible summaries. If it is a tape or a video, run it through completely in a relaxed state, in order to get the general outline, rather than the details. Do not jump to any conclusions, but wait until you have studied the lesson in depth.

Note what you know You might find it helpful at this stage to jot down, possibly in the form of a mind map, what you already know about the subject and what you hope to find out. This could be done before or after you have got your overview, depending on your familiarity with the subject.

Break it into 'chunks' If the subject you are about to study seems complex and lengthy, break it down into small and manageable sub-units or chunks. The brain can absorb an infinite amount of information, provided it is broken into amounts which it can digest. In this respect the brain is rather like the stomach.

Annotate and highlight Try to acquire your own copy of the important course books, so that you can mark them as you wish. To make your reading active, use coloured highlighter pens, write notes in the margin and draw pictures. This helps your memory and understanding.

Pause and summarize At the end of each learning section pause, reflect and make a summary. This can be in the form of a mind map (see below), or you can make a verbal summary, as if you were explaining the material to someone. You might be able to ask a friend to listen to you in the capacity of a student. You might also find it useful to write key words or phrases on Post-it notes or record cards. You can place these on the walls to act as reminders or take the cards with you to revise at odd moments during the day.

Use mind maps[1] Examples of mind maps are given at the end of each chapter of this book. They are 'brain friendly', in the sense that the brain stores information by association, in clusters , not in linear form. For this reason mind maps are easy to remember. Use key words, not sentences, and print them in capitals. Enhance with colours, illustrations and symbols. Show connections. Test yourself by creating a new mind map without reference to notes.

Mind maps make revision easier and quicker. Keep them in an indexed file and revise them regularly.

Visualize At the end of a learning session, relax and review what you have learned in your mind's eye. Note down anything which is unclear or cannot be recalled in detail. Try to add some human interest and feeling to the pictures you create.

Take regular breaks To maintain concentration and energy, stop every 40 minutes or so and do an energy-raising activity from Brain Gym or Office Yoga (see

Chapter 9). Alternatively, take a walk, breathing deeply, or make yourself a refreshing beverage (preferably not coffee (see Chapter 9 on diet)).

Use all your intelligences

You have at least seven intelligences, all of them capable of being developed by practise. They are not fixed at birth, as was thought in the past. They are simply a set of abilities and skills. They are listed in Chapter 8. The following are some hints on how to identify them in yourself, how to make use of them when studying and how to strengthen them for learning:

1 **Linguistic intelligence**[2]
   - *Likely traits*: You appreciate plays, poetry, books and conversation. You are a fluent talker and can explain things clearly.
   - *How to use when studying*: Make as much use as possible of language, both written and spoken. Read books. Write notes. Put your thoughts into words. Explain your ideas to others.
   - *How to strengthen for learning*: Tell or write stories, play memory games, keep a journal, do crosswords and word games.

2 **Logical/mathematical intelligence**
   - *Likely traits*: You like abstract thinking and are good at solving puzzles and problems. You know how to analyse and interpret data.
   - *How to use when studying*: Arrange tasks in a logical, orderly sequence. Look for patterns and relationships.
   - *How to strengthen for learning*: Practise solving problems. Do mathematical computation games. Analyse and interpret data.

3 **Visual-spatial intelligence**
   - *Likely traits*: You think in pictures and create visual images. You are observant and have a good sense of direction. You use metaphors.
   - *How to use when studying*: Make as much use as possible of films, slides and videos. Use charts, diagrams and mind maps. Put peripheral stimuli (such as posters containing learning material) on the walls.
   - *How to strengthen for learning*: Practise observing things which others do not notice. Play games like Pelmanism (remembering the position of cards placed face downwards on a table) or Kim's game (placing objects on a table and trying to recall them when they are covered with a cloth). Use mime. Practise visualizing.

4 **Musical intelligence**
   - *Likely traits*: You are sensitive to the emotional power of music and possibly also to its complex organization. You have a good sense of rhythm and/or melody. You remember songs and may be able to sing.
   - *How to use when studying*: Learn through songs. Compose your own jingles. Study while listening to Baroque music, possibly recording material on tape with such music in the background.

Change your mood with music. Use music to help you relax and/
or visualize.

- *How to strengthen for learning*: Learn to play a musical instrument, such as the guitar. Compose music on a computer. Attend concerts or listen with full attention to radio broadcasts of orchestral performances. Join a choir or choral group.

5 **Bodily/kinesthetic intelligence**
- *Likely traits*: You like engaging in physical sports. You prefer to deal with problems in a physical, 'hands on' way. You are skilful with your hands. You play around with objects while listening. You fidget if there are few breaks.
- *How to use when studying*: Use physical encoding exercises, imagining that you are the object you are learning about. Move around while learning. Act out the learning. Take lots of breaks, carrying out a physical activity, such as Brain Gym or Office Yoga. Mentally review while you are jogging, swimming or cycling.
- *How to strengthen for learning*: Learn Karate, Tai Chi, Yoga, circle dancing or any activity which improves your coordination and awareness of your body. Write a journal (writing is a kinesthetic activity and helps you clarify your thinking). Join an amateur dramatic society and practise acting (this will show you how memorizing lines is helped by physical actions).

6 **Inter-personal or 'social' intelligence**
- *Likely traits*: You relate well and like mixing with other people. You have many friends. You are good at negotiating. You enjoy group activities and you like to cooperate.
- *How to use when studying*: Do learning activities cooperatively. Arrange discussion groups about the subject being studied or about problems which arise. Take lots of breaks and socialize. Make learning fun.
- *How to strengthen for learning*: Attend parties and social functions. Take part in club activities. Talk to people. Help others with learning difficulties. Become interested in how others think and feel.

7 **Intra-personal or intuitive intelligence**
- *Likely traits*: You appreciate privacy and quiet for working and thinking. You like to daydream, imagine and fantasize. You understand your own feelings and thoughts and why you do things.
- *How to use when studying*: Discover the human interest background to whatever you are studying. Become involved emotionally. Discover the subject's personal significance to you. Take time for inner reflection. Listen to your intuition. Write down your thoughts. Study independently whenever possible.
- *How to strengthen for learning*: Hold inner dialogues with yourself. Learn and practise meditation. Keep a journal and use it to explore

your thoughts or to create imaginary dialogues with historical figures or experts in your field. Put aside time for review and reflection at the end of each day.

Memorize   Unless you have an unusually retentive memory, you will have to take some active steps to memorize important facts, names or figures relating to your subject.

The key elements of memory are as follows.

Original awareness   You must focus your full attention on the subject for long enough for your conscious mind to become fully aware of it. Try if possible to become aware of it with all your senses. If it is a name, see it in written form, possibly accompanied by a picture (visual), hear it spoken, either by yourself or by another person or on a tape (auditory) and say and write it, possibly while you are moving (kinesthetic).

Association   Try to find a link or association between the new knowledge and something similar which is already fixed in your memory. This can be either a clear, logical link or an artificial one, known sometimes as a mnemonic. For example, if you wanted to remember that the name of your company chairperson was Fisher, you might see her in your mind's eye leaning out of her office window with a fishing rod in her hand (a logical connection). If, however, her name was Reddux, the name has no inherent meaning. But you can give it one by spelling it phonetically. So Reddux becomes 'Red Ducks'. Now you can visualize the chairperson feeding some red ducks on the window sill of her office.

Visualization   To make the mental pictures mentioned above effective, it may be necessary to develop the skill of visualization. Just as you used as many senses as possible to create original awareness of the object you want to memorize, so you can use these same senses to make your mental picture clearer and more memorable. So try to create a picture in your mind which has colour, movement and detail. If possible bring in sounds. You may also be able to imagine yourself physically involved in some way with the action. Visualization is usually easier if you are in a relaxed state, so, if possible, find yourself a quiet environment and carry out some relaxation exercises (see Chapter 9) before starting to create your mental images.

There are a number of other memory techniques which can be useful when studying. These include the 'Loci System', the 'Chain of Links', the 'T for 1' system, and creating sentences in which the initial letter of each word stands for words which are to be remembered. They are described in Michael Lawlor's book *Inner Track Learning*.[3]

Another technique, which is particularly effective when learning languages, is to have the material recorded on tape with a background of Baroque music. This has the effect of inducing a state of enjoyable relaxation, which is optimal for receptive learning. Language courses using this method are available in French, German, Spanish and Italian from Accelerated Learning Systems Ltd.[4]

After the study session

It is unrealistic to expect to have mastered or memorized a subject without checking your knowledge and regular revision.

Some suggested steps are as follows.

Test yourself

Try to create a new mind map without referring to your original one or your notes. Then compare it with the original and revise incorrect or missing information.

Another method of self-testing is to make up flash cards, with a stimulus on one side and the answer on the other. This is particularly useful when learning a language or formulae, such as used in the moulding and firing of pots. An enjoyable and absorbing way of using these cards is to lay five of them out in a row, as if you were playing patience, with the stimulus (e.g., the word in your own language) uppermost and the material to be remembered on the under side. You take the first card on the left and see if you can remember the information given on the back. If you can, you move the card up to start a second row. If you cannot remember, you place the card on the right-hand end of the first row and try the next card. In this way you build up five rows of five cards, testing your knowledge of each card before moving it up to the next row.

You can also make up an index box, dividing it into sections. The first section contains cards with new words, with which to test yourself. If you can give the correct answer, you move the card to the second section. If you cannot, you place it at the back of the first section. The next day you test yourself on the cards in the second section, moving them on to a third section if you are successful or back to the first section if not. After a week you test yourself on the cards in the third section, moving them on to a fourth and final section if successful and back to the first section if not. The cards in the fourth section can be worked through after a month and then placed in a separate box for revision as and when the information is likely to be needed, as in the case of an examination. But by this time they should be in the long-term memory.

Some other ways of testing yourself are:

- Draw a flow chart of a process or series of actions which need to be carried out in sequence.
- Create a mental video film of what you have just learned.
- Dictate a verbal summary of what you have learned onto a tape recorder (either imaginary or real).

- Write a detailed entry in your journal of what you have just learned.

Bear in mind that any mistakes you make are part of the learning process and are valuable feedback, so do not get annoyed with yourself if you make them. Think of mistakes as stepping stones, not as stumbling blocks.

Whatever method you use, remember that regular revision or use is vital if you want the information to be available to you immediately, whenever you want it.

Teach it As the old adage says: 'The best way to learn something is to teach it'. Find a colleague, friend or member of your family who is willing to act as a student, and teach them what you have learned. Use visual, auditory and kinesthetic means of instruction. Try giving them a guided visualization. Imagine you are trying to create in your 'student' enthusiasm for the subject.

Practise

Mental rehearsal Create a mental 'video' of yourself putting into practice what you have learned. Start by looking at the picture from the outside, as if you were a spectator, i.e. you see yourself in the film. Then step inside your body and experience it kinesthetically. Repeat to yourself an affirmation that you can do it.

Role play If you are learning a physical skill or something like a language which involves interaction with other people, act it out physically, imagining the other person opposite you. This will give you confidence when you have to use the knowledge in real life.

Use it It is only when you have actually used the new knowledge in the real world that you can really say that you own it. So take every opportunity you can of becoming involved with activities which call for the use of your new knowledge.[5]

Notes and references

1 Mind Map is a registered trade mark of Tony Buzan. See, Buzan, T. (1993) *The Mind Map Book*, BBC Books, London.
2 See, Dryden, A. and Voss, J. (1993) *The Learning Revolution* (Chapter 10), Profile Books, Auckland, New Zealand. This is available from Accelerated Learning Systems Ltd. (see Appendix D for address).
3 Lawlor, M. (1988) *Inner Track Learning*, Pilgrims Publications, Kemble. This is available from the Forge House Centre (see Appendix D for address).
4 See Appendix D for address of Accelerated Learning Systems Ltd.
5 Some other useful books on study skills are as follows:
Ansell, G. (1984) 'Make the Most of your Memory', National Extension College Trust, Ltd., Cambridge, UK.
Beaver, D. (1994) *Lazy Learning*, Element Books Ltd., Shaftesbury, Dorset.

This books shows how NLP can be used for learning.

Buzan, T. (1988) *Make the Most of your Mind*, Pan Books, London.

Casey, F. (1985) *How to Study—A Practical Guide*, Macmillan Education Ltd., Basingstoke.

Downes, S. and Perry, P. (1983) *Improve your Learning*, Longman Group Ltd. and Manpower Services Commission, Harlow, Essex.

Dudley, G. (1986) *Double Your Learning Power*, Thorsons Publishing Group, Wellingborough, Northants.

Elliott, K. and Wright, D. (publication undated) *Studying the Professional Way—The OUTPUT Study Method*, Northwick Publishers, Worcester.

Good, M. and South, C. (1988) *In the know—8 keys to successful learning*, BBC Books, London.

Marshall, L. and Rowland, F. (1981) *A Guide to Learning Independently*, The Open University Press, Milton Keynes.

Meredeen, S. (1988) *Study for Survival and Success—Guidenotes for College Students*, Paul Chapman Publishing Ltd., London.

Ostrander, S. and Schroeder, L. (1995) *Superlearning 2000*, Souvenir Press, London.

Palmer, R. and Pope, C. (1984) *Brain Train—Studying for Success*, E. & F.N. Spon, London.

Rose, C. (1985) *Accelerated Learning*, Accelerated Learning Systems, Ltd., Aylesbury.

Rowntree, D. (1983) *Learn how to study—A programmed guide for students of all ages*, Macdonald & Co. Ltd., London.

A package entitled 'Accelerate Your Learning' containing three books, a video and an audio cassette is available from Accelerated Learning Systems Ltd. (see Appendix D for address).

Mind map for Chapter 15—study skills (2)

Transforming the organization

16 Creating

Scene *Jack Bird's office at Glospot Ltd. Jack, his brother Warren, and Tony Wakemen were sitting in comfortable chairs in a corner of the office, drinking coffee. There was a vase of flowers on the table and several attractive paintings of Japanese and Greek pots on the walls.*

'Warren and I have asked you to come and have a chat,' began Jack, 'because we're beginning to think you've got something with this new method of yours—it was since that session on visualization you did last week.'

'The fact is,' said Warren, 'Jack and I realize that we can't go on like this— not if we want the company to grow. You see Jack and I . . . well, we seem to be at each other's throats.'

'So you want me to help?' said Tony. 'Well, you've already taken the first step—realizing that you want to change.'

'Okay, now that it's out in the open, what can we do about it?' asked Jack abruptly.

'I think we need to look at this as an opportunity for some creative thinking,' replied Tony. 'Let's get your outcome clear. How exactly do you want your relationship to be?'

'Well, speaking for myself,' said Warren, 'I'd like to feel that Jack and I could discuss any problems that crop up in a way which didn't lead to an almighty row.'

'Could you put that in a more positive way?' asked Tony. 'Rather than thinking of what you want to avoid, think of how you would really like to relate to Jack. Imagine you are an observer, looking at the two of you meeting in, say, two month's time. What would the body language of the two of you look like? How *would your voices sound? What sort of language would you be using? Why don't you both close your eyes for a moment and imagine the scene?'*

Both men closed their eyes. As Tony watched, he detected a faint smile appearing on both their faces.

'It looks as if you like what you saw,' said Tony. 'Now I'd like you to close your eyes again and imagine that you are the same observer, but this time looking at the two of you having one of your usual confrontations. See it in detail, with full sound effects.'

The two men again closed their eyes. This time there was clearly tension in their faces and bodies.

'So you've now created two pictures,' said Tony. 'One of the vision of the future that you want and one of the present unwanted situation—I'd like you to bring them both into your mind at the same time . . . How does it feel?'

'Uncomfortable,' replied Warren at once. Jack nodded in agreement.

'Exactly,' said Tony. 'But this discomfort provides exactly what you need to motivate you to get where you want to go. It's called structural tension.'

What the two brothers have been exploring with Tony is the process of creating a desired outcome. This is a process which can be applied in any situation where the current reality of that situation does not correspond to how you would like it to be. It can be used to transform a personal relationship, as in this case, to set a new direction for an organization, as in the case of Glospot, or to deliver outstanding training events, as in the case of you as a trainer.

The process involves the use of both the left, logical brain and the right, imaginative brain. It is essentially a matter of having a clear mental picture or vision of the outcome you want to achieve and believing that you have the ability to create it. You adopt an orientation towards life which is essentially creative, rather than reactive.[1] This vision of your future outcome is not, however, enough by itself. It needs to be accompanied by a recognition of where you are now—your current reality. If these two pictures are held together in your mind, they create a feeling of discomfort. This arises from the opposition between the two conditions. They are like opposite poles.

Opposite electrical poles are known as positive and negative and they generate tension. This tension is resolved by the flow of electricity along the conductor which connects them. In the same way, the opposite poles of the future vision and the current reality generate tension which has to be resolved. It is known as structural tension. This tension can be used as the driving force which leads to the realization of a future vision.

Generating structural tension

The following are some suggested steps in the process of creating a desired outcome by means of generating structural tension. Let us imagine that you are a trainer and you have to give the key-note speech at a conference of traditional training officers from various government departments.

Define

The first thing is to be absolutely clear about what you really want. You need to take time to reflect on the outcome and to make sure that it is in accordance with your values and your long-term life goals. It should, to put it in NLP terms, be a 'well-formed' outcome.[2] This means that it should meet the following criteria.

Positive

The outcome should be positive. Think of what you want, rather than what you do not want. So instead of saying to yourself 'I want to avoid making a fool of myself in front of 300 experienced training officers', you might say 'I want to enthuse and transform 300 training officers'. To open up the possibility of more than one approach, you might like to change this to 'In what ways can I . . .?'

Own part

Think of what you can actively do that is within your control. Be aware that unless you envisage, plan and execute, the desired outcome will not happen.

Specific

Imagine the outcome as specifically as you can. Create in your mind a picture which contains colour, movement, detail and sound. See it from the point of view of the audience and from a neutral observer. Step inside your body and feel it.

Evidence

Ask yourself how you will know that you have achieved your outcome. What will you see, hear and feel?

Resources

What resources will you need to achieve your outcome? Do you know enough about the venue, or should you visit it in advance? What equipment will you need? Have you got all the information you will require? Have you allowed enough time for the preparation and copying of handouts?

Size

Ask yourself if the outcome is the right size. If it is too large, you should ask yourself 'What prevents me from getting this?' You might, for instance, think that addressing a plenary session of 300 highly experienced and senior training officers might be a task which is too big for you to take on. If this is the case, you may need to look at your belief system and perhaps go back in your memory to instances of challenges which you have responded to successfully.

If the outcome is too small, for instance if you only had a handful of people booked in for a workshop, you might like to ask 'If I got this outcome, what would it do for me?'. You might become aware that the experience you would gain and the influence you would exert would be sufficient motivation for you to go ahead with the workshop and give it your best.

Ecology frame   Check the consequences in your life and relationships if you achieved your outcome. Ask yourself 'What would happen if I got it?'. In this case, you might perhaps want to consider what the effect on your colleagues would be if you were a brilliant success and suddenly found yourself in demand as a speaker at large conferences. How would your family react if this meant your frequent absence from home?

Germinate   The next stage is to allow your subconscious mind to start germinating ideas. Now that you have a clear picture of a well-formed outcome, you can use it to allow ideas to be generated without conscious effort. Before going to sleep at night, place a sheet of paper and a pencil beside your bed. Allow a picture of the outcome to form in your mind. When you wake up in the morning write down any ideas, or possibly dreams, that relate to the achieving of the outcome. Keep a note book in your pocket throughout the day and jot down any ideas that occur to you. If possible continue this process for several days.

Cultivate   Find a quiet place where you will not be interrupted. Carry out some of the Brain Gym and relaxation exercises described in Chapter 9. Sit silently for at least 10 minutes and allow your mind to wander freely around the realization of your outcome. You might find that playing some Baroque or other relaxing music will help you to become more relaxed and imaginative. Take a large sheet of blank paper and some coloured felt tip pens and write in capital letters in the middle of it two words that summarize your desired outcome. Then, as ideas come to you, print them in different colours around the page, illustrate them if you wish, put a circle round each one and join it to the centre. Draw lines linking any ideas that seem to go together.

Stimulate   If you are still short of ideas, try some of the following techniques for stimulating more creative thinking.

Forcing connections   Look around you, either indoors or outside, and select an object, such as a tree. Take a piece of paper and draw a vertical line down the middle. In the left-hand column list the qualities of the object. Opposite each one, in the right-hand column, list any ideas which relate to the achieving of your outcome. In this case your list might look something like this:

Qualities of a tree   *Related ideas*

Rooted   Need the audience be rooted to their chairs? Could

	I get them to move around? Could I move around and interact with them?
Grows in woods	Make the audience feel they are part of a whole. Work in pairs or small groups. Do some group stretches.
Grows to maturity	Give the participants techniques for personal growth.
Provides shade	Emphasize caring and counselling role of trainer.
Bends in wind	Be flexible. Find out participants' needs and adapt talk accordingly.
Is colourful	Use colour in OHP foils and flip charts. Put up colourful peripherals. Use colourful speech images and metaphors.
Is peaceful	Give time for quiet reflection on theme.

Brainstorming   Work with a colleague or group of colleagues and brainstorm ideas for achieving the outcome. One person should write the ideas on a flip chart, possibly in the form of a mind map. Remember the main rule of brainstorming—there should be no critical comment on any idea.

Outlandish ideas   Deliberately think of bizarre, foolish, absurd or humorous ideas. Possible ideas for this case include: everyone coming in fancy dress; having the talk delivered by a clown; putting the talk to music and singing it with a guitar; forming mini-groups and asking someone in the group to give their version of what they think your talk is going to be about; sending everyone out on a treasure hunt; clearing the chairs away and having party games.

Examine any thinking blocks   These blocks may be:

- **Conceptual**. Have you considered all the possible sensory channels for delivering your message—auditory, visual, kinesthetic, tactile, olfactory, gustatory?
- **Emotional**. Is fear holding you back from trying out something which might have a big impact?
- **Cultural**. Do you know enough about the culture of your audience to assume that a particular approach might or might not work? Can you find out?
- **Thinking language**. Have you explored fully the possibilities of writing down your thoughts, illustrating them, dictating them onto a tape recorder or articulating them to someone else?

Plan   The time has come to sit down and sift through the various ideas and produce a plan, in this case a plan of your presentation. It can be linear at first, with exact timings and then perhaps in the form of a colourful mind map for quick reference. You may have more than one plan, in which case you will have to carry out the next step—to choose.

Choose If you have several alternative plans, you will have to choose which one to adopt. The best way to do this is to allocate points to each one, based on the criteria you adopted to establish your outcome.

Decide Now comes the moment of decision. You must opt for one of the plans and make a firm mental decision to go ahead with it.

Prepare You do everything you have to do to put into effect the plan you have decided on. You do it in good time to allow for things going wrong and to avoid any sense of rush or pressure.

Energize This is where the concept of structural tension, mentioned at the beginning, comes in. Sit down, relax and create two mental pictures— one of the desired outcome and the other of the current reality. Become aware of the gap between them and experience structural tension. State clearly your choice between the two and allow your attention to rest on the picture of the outcome. For a full description of this process see *The Path of Least Resistance* by Robert Fritz.

Act Go for it—put your plan into action, inspired by your vision and by the knowledge that you have chosen the best plan possible for you.[3]

Notes and references

1 See, Fritz, R. (1989) *The Path of Least Resistance—Learning to become the Creative Force in your own Life*, Fawcett Columbine, NY USA.
2 See, O'Connor, J. and Seymour, J. (1993) *Introducing Neuro-Linguistic Programming* (pp. 13–14), Aquarian Press, Wellingborough.
3 The following books on creative thinking and problem solving are also recommended for further reading:
Adams, J. (1987) *Conceptual Blockbusting—A Guide to Better Ideas*, Penguin Books, London.
Bono, E. de (1982) *de Bono's Thinking Course*, BBC Books, London and subsequent books by the same author.
Evans, R. and Russell, P. (1989) *The Creative Manager*, Unwin Paperbacks, London.
Hopson, B. and Scally, M. (1989) *Wake Up Your Brain—Creative Problem Solving*, Lifeskills, Leeds.
Nierenberg, G. (1982) *The Art of Creative Thinking*, Simon & Schuster, New York USA.
Nolan, V. (1987) *The Innovator's Handbook*, Sphere Books Ltd., London.
Oech, R. von (1983) *A Whack on the Side of the Head*, Angus & Robertson Publishers, London.
Olson, R. (1978) *The Art of Creative Thinking*, Barnes & Noble Books, New York USA.

Mind map for Chapter 16—creating

17 Towards a learning organization

Yet all experience is an arch wherethro'
Gleams that untrav'lled world, whose margin fades
For ever and for ever when I move

from *Ulysses* by
Alfred, Lord Tennyson

Scene *The kafenio on the beach at Chryssopigi on the island of Sifnos. Jill Bird and her friend, Angelos, are sipping glasses of ouzo and admiring the sunset.*

'Well,' said Angelos. 'Tell me about it. How did the handover go?'

Jill gazed at the crimson glow in the sky, as the sun slid towards the horizon.

'It was a great farewell,' she said. 'I think Glospot is in safe hands. Warren and Jack have patched up their differences. More than that. They seem to have become friends. They've agreed to rotate the running of the business. One of them will look after the shop for a year while the other will be in Japan. Then they'll swap.'

'Japan?' asked Angelos.

'Yes. You know Warren used to import Japanese paintings. He's been to Japan a few times and knows the scene there quite well. He's discovered that the Japanese are mad about English gardens. And they need English garden pots. Large ones. Like the ones we make. So he's setting up a very profitable business supplying the Japanese market. And we're also importing some high quality Japanese porcelain and selling it in our new visitors' centre.'

'Visitors' centre? What's happening to dear old Glospot?'

'I think it's undergoing a metamorphosis. I can't really take any credit. It's all due to that young man we recruited—Tony Wakeman. He set up a training programme which got everyone interested in improving their job performance.

And he taught us how to visualize. We worked out a vision for the future of the company, getting people at all levels to contribute. It was amazing how many ideas came out. We've got enough to last for years. I've invited him to join the board.'

'And you finally decided to step down, Jill. I'm so glad.'

'Only partly, I'm afraid, Angelos. I'm becoming the company chairman—or chairperson as the young people want to call me. There are some exciting ideas which I intend to take part in developing.'

'Such as?'

'Well, the most important is to turn Glospot into a learning organization.'

'A learning organization? What could that be?'

'That, my dear Angelos, is another story.'

The sun had disappeared, leaving the sea as Homer had described it—wine dark. Jill had a feeling that her odyssey was at an end. Or was it, she wondered, just beginning?

The logic of the approaches to training described in the previous chapters of this book leads to the creation of a learning organization. What exactly is a learning organization?

The following is one of several current definitions:

> A learning organization is one which facilitates the learning of all its members and continuously transforms itself.' (Pedler, Boydell and Burgoyne)[1]

The concept is a relatively new one and there is no clearly marked and tried path leading to it. However, a widely accepted description is given in Peter Senge's *The Fifth Discipline*[2] and some detailed guidelines are given in the subsequent *The Fifth Discipline Field Book*.[3] A number of the training skills described in *The Creative Trainer*[4] relate directly to Peter Senge's five disciplines. The link between them is explained briefly below.

Personal mastery (The first discipline)

Personal mastery is a concept based on Robert Fritz's Technologies for Creating.[5] It means changing from a reactive–responsive to a creative orientation towards life. Instead of allowing outside circumstances to determine your behaviour, you decide to become the creative force in your life.

The technique for doing this is based on visualization. To start with you become clear about your aim. You visualize a clear multi-sensory image of it and then compare this with things as they are now—your current reality. Holding these two images together produces structural tension. To resolve this tension you have to decide to move either in the direction of the future vision or to return to the status quo—the current reality. The acceptance of the reality of the present situation and the decision to move away from it is like changing the structure of the terrain in which a river is flowing. The water will change direction because it follows the path of least resistance.

Visualization is described in Chapter 13 and the process of creating structural tension is described in Chapter 16. So the basic building block of the five disciplines of the learning organization will already be familiar to you.

Mental models (The second discipline)

By mental models is meant the way in which you see and interpret the world. There are many people who are firmly convinced that their interpretation of the world, their 'map', is the same as the world outside, the 'territory'. The fact is that everyone makes their own mental map and no two maps are exactly the same. By examining the way in which your own mental map was constructed, you become aware of beliefs which may be ill-founded and you become open to more choices. You also realize how other people's maps differ from your own and thus become better able to communicate with them.

In Chapter 8 you will have seen how your brain dominance determines your thinking and learning style. Awareness of the brain quadrant or quadrants which you habitually use will enable you to explore other ways of thinking and to understand better the points of view of other people.

Shared vision (The third discipline)

A shared vision is one that people in an organization are committed to, because it reflects their own personal vision. When people share a vision they are connected; bound together by a common aspiration. Shared vision is vital for an organization because it provides a focus and energy for learning.

As in the case of personal mastery, shared vision is based on the skill of visualization, which is described in Chapter 13.

Team learning (The fourth discipline)

Team learning is the process of aligning and developing the capacity of a team to create results which its members truly desire. It builds on the disciplines of shared vision and personal mastery. Personal mastery without shared vision is likely to produce a chaotic situation with all the members pulling in opposite directions. The aim of team learning is to tap the potential of many minds to be more intelligent than just the sum of each individual mind. This is known as synergy.

Figure 17.1 *... those engaged in dialogue must agree to suspend their assumptions and to regard one another as colleagues, rather than adversaries. A facilitator is normally needed to see that the rules of dialogue are observed ...*

The fundamental skill to master in team learning is that of dialogue, as opposed to discussion. Whereas discussion tends to be confrontational, dialogue involves listening and results in a free and creative exploration of issues. There is a flow of meaning. Those engaged in dialogue must agree to suspend their assumptions and to regard one another as colleagues, rather than adversaries. A facilitator is normally needed to see that the rules of dialogue are observed. Creating the right atmosphere for dialogue depends to a large extent on a positive group dynamic. How this can be created is described in Chapters 3 to 7—the four-quadrant creative trainer teaching cycle.

Systems thinking (The fifth discipline)

Systems thinking is the conceptual cornerstone of the other four disciplines. It is essentially about seeing wholes. It is a framework of inter-relationships rather than isolated events. It is based on the twin concepts of feedback from cybernetics and servo-mechanisms from engineering theory. It is a discipline for seeing the structures that underlie complex situations. It is about perceiving points of leverage, where a small action can have a significant effect.

In Senge's systems thinking model, it is the outside structure and conditions which determine events and the decisions which flow from them (see his description of the Beer Game in Chapter 3 of *The Fifth Discipline*). The skill of systems thinking is to be able to see that events in time are not linear but linked to each other in feedback loops.

This concept has much in common with the behavioural model proposed by Robert Fritz in his *Technologies for Creating*. According to Fritz's model, structure determines the path of least resistance and decides to a large extent the path which people follow in their lives. However, it is the structure within the mind which determines action, rather than the outside conditions. It is this which guides the direction in which the energy of the individual will flow—either towards a future vision or back to the current reality. Fritz calls this phenomenon structural tension, his concept of which is described in Chapter 16 of this book.

We hope that you have enjoyed reading this book and that you have found some useful ideas. Basically, the ideas you have read about can be no more than the ingredients, out of which you can mix and bake your own cake, or the tubes of paint which you can squeeze onto your palette and create your own picture. For, as its name implies, the purpose of the book is to help you to apply your innate ability to create to the task of training and becoming a true facilitator.

If you think of each training session which you run, not as a routine task, but as an opportunity to be creative, your life will be enriched. You will experience the excitement and fulfilment of the creative artist—the painter, the sculptor or the writer. But, unlike them, you will have the enrichment and stimulus of interacting with people and of knowing then and there that you have made a difference in their lives. You will not have to wait, perhaps for years, for your work to be appreciated. You will know at once. You will see it in the faces of your course participants. You will hear it in their voices, perhaps even in the sound of their applause. You will feel it at the deepest level of your being. There is nothing quite like it.

Good luck.

Notes and references

1 Pedler, M., Burgoyne, J. and Boydell, T. (1991) *The Learning Company*, McGraw-Hill, Maidenhead, Berks.

2 Senge, P. (1990) *The Fifth Discipline—The Art and Practice of the Learning Organization*, Century Business Books, London.

3 Senge, P., Roberts, C., Ross, R., Smith, B. and Kleiner, A. (1994) *The Fifth Discipline Fieldbook—Strategies and Tools for Building a Learning Organization*, Doubleday, New York USA.

4 *The Creative Trainer* (Chapter 16).

5 A method developed by Robert Fritz and described in Fritz, R. (1989) *The Path of Least Resistance—Learning to become the Creative Force in your Own Life*, Fawcett Columbine, New York USA.

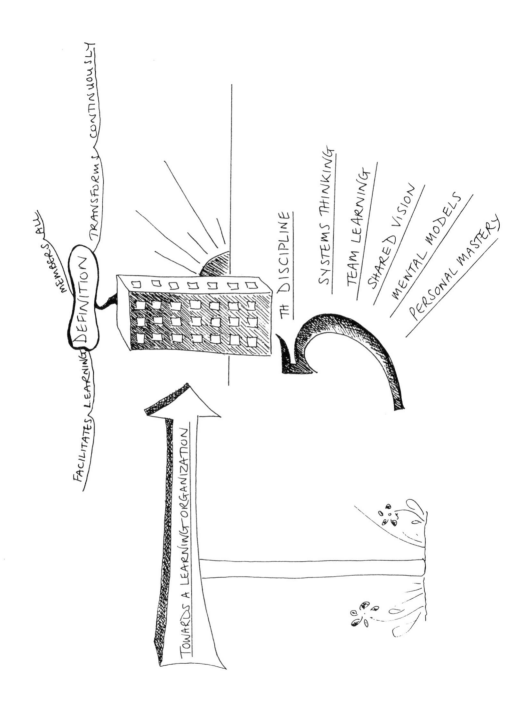

Mind map for chapter 17—towards a learning organization

PART 6

The method in action

18 Case studies

It's difficult to say what is impossible, for the dream of yesterday is the hope of today and the reality of tomorrow

R.H. Goddard

Case study 18.1 Allied Dunbar

Allied Dunbar is a large financial services company based in Swindon, Wiltshire. Approximately 3000 staff are employed in Swindon, with about 300 branches throughout the country and in excess of 4000 sales associates.

Allied Dunbar started business in 1971 with £1 million capital. Its aim was to find a new way of doing business in the insurance sector. The company was floated on the stock exchange in 1976 and after consistent growth was acquired by BAT Industries for £660 million.

Quality is one of the key issues the company aims to keep high in its priorities. During 1989 and 1990 a large number of staff participated in Total Quality Management programmes, with quality circle meetings[1] being encouraged for the staff to find ways to improve how they did their jobs.

As a part of the financial services industry over the past few years, the company has seen increased competition from various sectors, the introduction of financial legislation and effects of the current recession.

Quality service continues to be a key initiative within Allied Dunbar and this is the basis for the work carried out by the company in improving letter writing standards.

The following case study is based on extracts from a conversation with Ian Hughes (IH) Training and Development Consultant at Allied Dunbar and Peter Handley (PH). The interview is designed to give you some background to the application of Accelerated Learning (AL) to an organizational training issue, using the four-stage model.

Ian first learned of Accelerated Learning by attending a workshop in the UK at the Kingwood Centre for Learning.

Introduction   PH: Why did you choose the AL concept for your course design and delivery?

IH: We knew intuitively and from a needs analysis point of view that we had a big job on our hands to shift, significantly, the quality of the letter writing in our Client Services Division.

PH: I imagine a straightforward training course might have served your needs?

IH: Yes, it would have been very easy to have run a course for managers to improve their ability to assess the quality and then run programmes subsequently for staff using traditional training techniques. However, we found letter writing to be a very sensitive area in terms of style and content for most people. So we had to find a way of changing people's attitudes and motivation while at the same time addressing skill improvement.

We chose the AL format because the number of people we had to train was in excess of 500; this format enabled us to train larger groups more quickly. We wanted to make the training different and we wanted to make the learning fun. Making it fun would certainly be a feature that would make it different from our traditional courses. Also, we wanted to get away from spelling tests, grammar exercises and learning by rote, which are usual with letter-writing courses. Most importantly, we wanted people to see that letter writing could be exciting, as some people saw letter writing as the least exciting part of their job.

Many people had become dependant on standard letters, produced by a computer, which at best they might modify or adapt, rather than writing a letter especially for a particular person. We wanted to improve the standards, through the managers, who would be responsible for the quality of letters sent to our clients.

PH: How did you prepare your learners for learning or improving the standards of letter writing?

Preparation   IH: We decided to start the event by having a pre-course quiz. So the joining instructions for the event actually contained a piece of written work that they had to try and find all the errors in—spelling, grammar, inconsistencies. There was also information about what we were going to do in parts one and two; the learner benefits they would expect to get from attending; a sense of what they would be able to do as a result. For example, they would be able to assess people's skill sets. Also there was information about how to prepare for the programme. The joining instructions were very well received and we got feedback from people saying how much they had liked them and how different they were.

PH: What room preparation did you plan in terms of preparing a welcoming environment?

IH: The room was not set out in a traditional style of a 'U' shape with projector and screen. Our people had already experienced 'café style' work groups, where there is no 'front of the room' approach. In fact, our trainers tend to sit in the room with the people. There was a theme to the room which came very late in the planning process. We wanted something that would reinforce the message that we were investing hundreds of thousands of pounds a year in our written communication, which in most cases was not reaching the standard.

The 'Postman Pat' image came to mind and the image we had of Postman Pat was someone who had lots of adventures while trying to deliver the mail. That was the start point. As the theme developed it became Postman Pratt and the reason that it seemed to work for us was that we were all being Postman Pratt writing these letters, sending them to people and in some cases only creating the need for the client to phone us to ask us questions to clarify what we had written. So the room had a large Postman Pratt theme with a postman outside welcoming people to the room. The room also had large posters in it, which were emphasizing some of the problems we knew we had in our communication. We had pictures or images that went along with that. We also had welcoming music, flowers on the tables, and everywhere looking very colourful.

PH: What happened when people actually came into the room?

IH: When people arrived we found that the pre-course exercise enabled people very quickly to discuss with each other their joining instructions and share how many mistakes they had found. This soon generated a feeling of collaboration rather than competition, simply by giving permission to people to compare and contrast their views.

PH: What other things did you do to generate a feeling of collaboration?

IH: We also asked people to bring with them examples of letters that they had received at home or at Allied Dunbar, which they regarded as being absolutely atrocious, and some they thought were really good. It would be their judgement. So we immediately went into a session where each table shared with each other their examples, telling each other why they thought each letter was awful or why they thought it was good. This was then fed back to the trainer who facilitated understanding of what constitutes good and bad standards.

PH: Tell me about the ways in which you presented the learning material.

Presentation

IH: One of the ways we used was to get everyone involved in the material. We gave everyone a pack of 10 letters and asked each person separately to rank them in order of quality. When that was done individually, we then asked them to discuss their ranking in their table groups and explore their differences and agreements.

This enabled us very quickly and collaboratively to get agreement on the standards we were implementing.

We also used a Rowan Atkinson tape to demonstrate waffle speaking. People in the group also volunteered some of the waffle letters that they had brought with them and read them out loud in a kind of dramatic reading to over-emphasize the point.

To put across the visual impact letters have on the recipient, we asked people to paste-up the letters that they had brought with them and then stand three metres back and select the one that they thought had the best visual impact. So we used that approach to get people to see that you judge a letter not just by what it says but how it looks when you take it out of the envelope.

Also on the staff course, what worked extremely well was the agony aunt column. We asked the participants to imagine that they were writing to Aunt Marjorie, the Letter Writing Agony Aunt. They could ask for help with anything to do with writing letters. All the problems were recorded on Post-it notes and the group worked on them individually and in their table groups. We then had a coffee break. While they were doing that we were able to assess each problem and relate them to the basic letter-writing process that we used on that course, which was plan your letter, write your letter and edit your letter. For example, one problem stated 'I don't know how to structure a letter', so we would classify that as a letter-planning problem. The next one might read 'I don't know how to start a letter' (again, a planning problem). Having posted all these problems, we were able to refer to them during the course and check back against them at the end of the day and say, have we covered all these problems? Have we dealt with them?

PH: Did you use concert reviews?

IH: No, however, we did use music in the second part of the programme, which linked the two programmes together. So when people came in to the second programme there was a strong memory association with the previous course.

PH: How did you accommodate all learning styles?

IH: We were using the whole range of learning techniques with very few didactic sessions. We also had exercises at different points in the course where people would get up and physically move around. The trainer could introduce these at will. They also served as an energizer, because where we had gone from a fairly didactic session about something conceptual, we were able to say, 'Well that's great, now let's explore that through this exercise'. So we would ask them in their table groups to look at how the particular concept that we had just been explaining works in practice. These exercises were energizing and motivating and they worked very well.

PH: How were the participants able to demonstrate their skills during the course?

Practice

IH: We had assessment criteria, which we used to judge the quality of our letters. So if we wanted our letter to be jargon- and waffle-free, we made people on the course responsible for each criteria. They could, for example, become 'jargon', 'spelling' or 'grammar'. They each received a badge that designated the criteria and they were instructed to become very clear, by studying the standards, about exactly what they were looking for. We also provided them with a rubber stamp for each criteria. They then went and examined each others' letters. If they found anything wrong, they had to stamp the letter and write below their stamp exactly why they felt it was wrong, with proposals about how they could improve it. If the problem was waffle they had to write a sentence or a phrase that would help clarify it. So we ended up with very senior managers wearing very large badges carrying a rubber stamp, marking-up all these letters and having great fun in the process. It was very active learning.

PH: Did you use articulation at all as a way of reinforcing learning?

IH: We used articulation to review and summarize the learning that had happened in a previous period. It is very common for us to say, 'We have just spent 40 minutes talking about that, now find a person in the room and explain to them as though they have never heard it before, what you have grasped about this particular concept'.

PH: Having given them time to practise, what design methods did you install to ensure consolidation of the new standards in the work performance?

Performance

IH: Remember these were managers whose requirement was to manage the standard of letter writing of their staff. So the requirement was that each manager would get 10 letters from each person reporting to them. From this they would make an assessment about each of the people reporting to them. They then had to show the results of this assessment to their peers. From that, they discussed the implications and strategy for bringing each person to the required standard. Part two of the course dealt specifically with these issues.

PH: Having been through the AL process or model, how would you sum up how this mode and philosophy of learning has helped to achieve the outcomes you wanted?

IH: I would sum it up like this: We got an improvement in performance as a result of the training intervention. We did not have a way of testing whether this was any better or worse than we could have got using more traditional methods. We did not run any parallel group using a different approach, although we do have an intuitive feel from our experience of tackling similar issues.

The benefit for us was that everyone was involved—trainers, participants, managers and the written communication team who were, in fact, the clients. I genuinely think that people got more fun out of it. There are some 600 people involved in this programme and for them it was a more pleasant experience in terms of putting 600 people through this kind of learning process than running programmes around grammar and so forth (which we did explore). The second thing in using the AL design model is that it genuinely led to an ability to work more creatively and come up with ideas that we think we would have not had otherwise.

Some of the experiences that people had, like the letter stamping exercise, were very memorable. It really did anchor the contents in people's minds about what the role of the learner was. So we were able to train a lot of people very quickly, typically running groups of 15 to 20 people at a time—half as much again as we would normally do. It was easy to adapt for particular groups of staff. Also the materials that we used were in fact given to us by the participants, so we were using material that was directly relevant to them.

As a total experience it was very productive and the design process was speeded up. All the course results exceeded our expectations on all fronts—to make the learning event different, to keep learning retention high, to be memorable and fun.

Case study 18.2 Robson Rhodes

Robson Rhodes is a leading firm of chartered accountants and management consultants and the UK member of RSM International, the world's tenth largest international association of accountants and management consultants.

The company provides a full range of high quality financial advisory services to help business maximize potential and profitability. It is a national firm in the UK, sharing profits, investments, resources and skills from one pool. This is just one of the factors that differentiates it from its principal competitors.

In 1987, the company developed a business strategy which drives its practice today. Client satisfaction and consistent high quality work are at the heart of this strategy. This has seen an increase in the number of prestigious clients and has accelerated the growth of its business.

Technical and professional standards are rigorously monitored by its in-house technical department, which is headed by a past member of the Accounting Standards Committee. A testament to its technical excellence and independence from conflicts of interest is that it is increasingly in demand by all the main financial regulatory authorities in the UK for review of the work of its competitors.

The business is managed by a management board, headed by the National Managing Partner. At the time of writing, the company has 73 partners and 407 professional staff in a total of 707 people. Against this background the firm has been encouraging its partners and professional staff to increase efficiency and productivity through the use of information technology. New methods of training were required to increase the motivation to computerized systems.

This case study looks at the way in which Nicky Shorey (NS), in her role as Head of Information Systems Training, undertook that challenge through the use of Accelerated Learning concepts applied to their Lotus 123 spreadsheet course. She talks to Peter Handley (PH).

Introduction

PH: What was it that led you towards considering the concept of Accelerated Learning for information technology courses in general?

NS: I wanted to make learning computers interesting and fun and I looked at many courses that I thought might help me. The course on AL looked exciting and interesting and seemed to be the answer.

PH: How was training done before you arrived at Robson Rhodes?

NS: There was no real formal training at all before I arrived. It was done on a one-to-one basis when someone had to use the computer. Generally people did not use computers widely in their job. They had to be shown just how much computers could improve their work practices.

PH: To summarize, then, there was no classroom-based training. What training there was, was done on a 'have to' basis, and only one-to-one, ad hoc, with people resisting learning computers. Then you arrived to bring about a formalized training strategy for the implementation of IT for the accountants and partners.

NS: Yes, that's about right.

PH: Had you run many computer courses before attending the AL course?

NS: Yes, I had. I guess intuitively I was already bringing colour into my training, and a bit of humour, trying to make people feel comfortable. So that when I heard the conceptual overview at the beginning of the AL course, everything just clicked with me. I was absolutely hooked. This was the right approach for me and for helping people to overcome their resistance to learning.

I went back to my boss and said 'I am going to revolutionize training here at Robson Rhodes. He said 'Okay', and then I went shopping for equipment to furnish the room. Two weeks later I knew I had a new course to present and the following is the result of the design of the Lotus 123 course for accountants with little or no experience of computers.

Preparation

PH: How did you prepare the learner for learning? Did you send a pre-course invitation?

NS: First of all, I had a theme in my mind for the course. I think I got the idea from someone on the AL course that I attended. I heard someone choose an oriental theme for the course. Not being one to reinvent the wheel, I thought that I would do that. I created a lot of oriental style peripherals, and I wanted the invitation to have an oriental style.

I have an oriental board game called 'Go' at home. The board on which you play looks very similar to the Lotus spreadsheet. To link the game to an oriental theme I invented two oriental characters. The invitation went out as if it was sent by these two people, inviting the participants to find out all about the game called 'Go' and its relationship with Lotus 123. It was very colourful, with little oriental pictures with positive learner suggestions and advice about how to get the best out of the workshop. Also inside was a bingo-style quiz, so anyone who had some knowledge could check their existing knowledge. Those who did not know, could ask others. It was not meant to be a test. I also gave them a diskette with a spreadsheet on it, with written instructions on how to load it. Then I gave them some 'go to' instructions on how to navigate around Lotus. All this was preparing them for something different. I have to say, that within the world of chartered accountancy the courses that they usually go on are very formal—very much 'chalk and talk'. I wanted to create a high level of interest, as a lot of them were not keen on getting computerized. At that time they saw computers as really something for secretaries, not as powerful business tools for themselves.

PH: What did you do in terms of creating a welcoming learning environment?

NS: I was very fortunate in that I had a room with natural daylight. I got a few people in the department to help with making colourful peripherals. We made various things about Lotus—key messages, saving files, etc. Everything had a very oriental feel to it.

We had room to train eight people at a time, so we had two big tables with two large screens on them. We had two people sitting one side and two people sitting the other side. We had flowers, coloured pens for the people to write or draw with, mints, and water to drink on a side table.

PH: What happened when people came into the room?

Presentation

NS: When everyone had sat down, I broke the ice by allaying some of their fears and concerns about the course. I gave them an overview of the course, which gave them the big picture—how they would succeed in terms of what they were going to achieve, and when the breaks would come. Then, by way of introducing the course members, I checked their expectations in terms of what they felt they were going to get out of the course by using the koosh ball. Throwing this soft ball to each other enabled each person in turn to speak about their expectations. These I listed on the flip chart in the form of a mind map.

PH: How did you get people into a collaborative frame of mind?

NS: The quiz they had been given with the joining instructions was used to make sure that everyone in the room had the same answers. They could do this quiz by making use of all the resources in the room. This meant working with everyone, not just at their table, and looking at everything that was available. Even my notes could be used if asked for.

PH: Now you were ready for the presentation of the learning inputs. What methods did you use?

NS: I taught in very small chunks. My inputs were short and I wanted to appeal to all learning styles. I used the following four stages:

1 I introduced the topic, and said what the benefits were, i.e. why we were doing this.
2 I then outlined the content of what we would be covering.
3 I explained how we would be practising the skills learned.
4 I outlined in what situations they could and would be using the spreadsheet exercises in their workplace.

The four stages follow David Kolb's Learning Cycle[2]. Generally speaking, I would explain the reasons for learning each part of the computer package, with explanations of the theoretical concepts behind them. Then I would demonstrate the process. I would do this by asking each person to do it with me, taking them through it once. Each person followed along with me as I demonstrated each part of the section of the computer programme. I would then give them an exercise to complete in pairs, e.g. to complete a formula change in the spreadsheet. Finally, I allowed them to have a little play with it, to see what situations they could apply it to from their own experience. And that would be the format of each lesson or small chunk in the computer programme.

At the end of each lesson, what I did was to get them in their pairs using those little Post-it notes to write a quiz question or two on the topic that they had just covered. It could be a question that they wanted to ask me at the time, or it could be a question like 'How do you save a file?', i.e. anything that was on their mind. I copied the idea of having a 'wizard board'. On the AL course, at the back of the room there was a poster and on it was a picture of a wizard. Underneath were written the words 'If you want to ask a question, ask the wizard. The wizard knows everything'. The idea being introduced was that all we had to do was write a question on a Post-it note and at the end of the day or session all the questions would be answered. And so it was with my Lotus course. Although I did not have a wizard board, I had an 'Ask Buddha board' as that sounded oriental and appropriate. So, at the end of each lesson we generated, say, five or six questions on that particular lesson topic, and that's how the day progressed.

PH: How did the participants react to this oriental theme?

NS: They were very cautious at first, but soon entered into the spirit of it. You see, I also provided rice crackers and green tea—something different to offer them at break times. We even managed on several occasions to get an oriental lunch in, as opposed to a standard buffet.

PH: How did you review the learning?

NS: At the end of the day I would do a concert review. The concert review would be my slides or flip charts, or pointing at the various peripherals around the room, with everyone sitting attentively relaxed, listening to Baroque music. After that we would have a team quiz based on the questions that they had generated during each lesson. Depending on how many people on the course, I would divide them into two or three teams. I had made something similar to a snakes and ladders board, but it had little oriental bits and pieces on it. They threw a die and if they got a question right they would go up the ladder. If they got it wrong, they would go down, etc. We kept this going throughout the three days and when we had run out of questions we would simply carry it over to the next day.

The fun that came out of the quiz was tremendous. It was non-threatening, team-based, and they could butt in and make silly noises, cut in on the other team if they did not know the answer, etc. It was a real hoot. They all said that they did not realize that they had covered so much.

PH: Were you able to use mnemonics to help people remember things?

NS: Yes. One particular one comes to mind: BODMAS. This enables people to remember how to use a formula. When you have to set up a formula in a spreadsheet you have to get the formula right in the first place, and Lotus, like any other spreadsheet, uses the same method of working out equations or formula. BODMAS stands for Brackets, any formula within brackets is calculated before the O (for Order) of Division, Multiplication, Addition and Subtraction. People remembered that easily.

PH: What other techniques did you use to get the material over?

NS: Because the theme was oriental, the exercises I used to help them grasp the concept were based in a Chinese restaurant where they worked out bills and VAT. I used short relaxation exercises before using guided imagery to take them in their imagination to a Chinese restaurant. In this way they could imagine that they were part of the restaurant. It was amazing just how much of an energizer it proved to be.

PH: To explain computer concepts, did you use any other learning methods?

NS: I mentioned earlier the oriental game, 'Go'. If you have ever seen this game you will know it is just a grid. It has numbers down one side and letters down the other. What I did was to explain the concept of how big the spreadsheet was. I got a piece of A4 paper and cut out a screen shape, placed the paper on top of the board and just moved it around a bit until they got the idea that there was much of the spreadsheet that they could not see. The concept was explained in seconds rather than minutes and was more memorable too.

To teach them the difference between relative and absolute addressing in Lotus was actually quite difficult. To help them understand I designed this massive spreadsheet like a carpet on the floor with a grid on it. In Lotus, each cell contains a formula which converts into an amount when a 'command' is given. I asked the participants to stand in the squares and act the parts—either as formulae or amounts. I asked something like, 'What is that formula saying? Now let someone else copy you elsewhere and what has to happen, and what needs to be changed, etc'. That worked very well. Again it was simple, easy to use, highly memorable, and people had a lot of fun with it.

PH: Tell me about the music. How did you use it, and when?

NS: I tried a little bit of oriental but mostly it was classical, acceptable music like Pachelbel, Vivaldi, Bach. I had it playing as they came into the room to set the scene. Every time they worked on their own or in pairs to explain something to each other that I had just talked about, I would put music on in the background. It was very well received. I got many comments about how it helped to make their learning less stressful and therefore more relaxing.

PH: You mentioned coloured pens earlier on. Was this for note taking or making mind maps?

NS: Some of them tried using these, but the note taking and the mind mapping were not so successful. So what I did was to give them a photocopied set of my overheads and a Lotus manual. My overheads were colourful, had the oriental theme, were image-orientated rather than word-based, and I said 'Do what you like with these overheads. If you want to make your own notes on them, please do so with the coloured pens provided'. I know that proved very popular and that it basically came about after reviewing mind mapping during a course review. I asked two questions 'What went well and what could have gone better?'. I brought that in after a couple of the reviews where the mind mapping did not seem to be going that well. So I thought, 'I will just give them my pictures (overheads), as pictures mean more and they remember them more'—especially if they are colouring them as well. When it came to the quiz, they remembered the pictures and the associated answers and they remembered where to look them up.

PH: Now we are into the practice phase. Can you tell some more about how you did that?

Practice

NS: Most of the time they were working in pairs. We did the articulation bit, where A describes to B their understanding of the concept that they had just performed. Also, one of the good things about working with computers is that you can ask them to demonstrate, i.e. 'show you know'. We had lots of exercises where they could do this after each short chunk of input and demonstration from me. One of the projects that they did in pairs was to create little help sheets for others in the group and then exchange them. I have mentioned the quiz that we used at the end of each day and that shows them, too, what they have learned.

PH: How did you make the transfer of learning to their own applications or in the workplace?

Performance

After each lesson section I would give time to each person to develop applications from their own job requirements. I would ask them how important that particular section was and get a few examples of how they might apply it. Then I would allow time for them to make the transfer to their work. They then could take this back to their workplace and develop it further. Some people brought work applications with them, like profit and loss accounts for their clients.

After they had completed the course, I sent them a reminder note of the key points of their learning. I also enclosed a photograph of the participants which I took during the course, at moments when they were obviously enjoying themselves or experiencing learning success. These two simple things serve as positive reminders of the learning event.

Summary

NS: I have to say that when I first started doing these courses, people who heard about them would say that you are not supposed to have fun on a training course. But after attending one, people found it very comfortable. I think that the spirit of AL is that you care that your learners learn. I do as much as I can to ensure that they get the learning that they want. That was the thing, whether consciously appreciated or not, that drew people to these courses, from all levels within the organization. It was a very joyful way of getting an organization to be very pro computers.

PH: Having had success with this course, what about your other courses?

NS: All my computer training is now in this format. In fact, I have now trained other trainers in AL. I think we have found the approach very flexible. I have such a rich supply of approaches and methods that I can choose which will help or assist the learners' ability to learn. Because that is what I care about. Whatever effort you put in, you get a huge reward because you see people relax and enjoy the learning experience.

I apply the 80/20 rule—20 per cent of the time I am leading, but 80 per cent is spent with the learner actively involved in their learning process by actually doing it!

PH: What about the evaluation of the course by course members?

NS: Reading course evaluation sheets stating how much they've enjoyed it and asking what other courses are offered is very encouraging for me. My boss at the time, who helped me introduce AL, happened to be travelling back to London on the train with a couple of senior partners who had come on my Lotus course. He had said to me that if you can get that particular individual (one of the senior partners travelling back) on your course he would give me the largest bunch of flowers that I had ever seen. He did come on the course and this is the statement he gave me on the evaluation form:

'I could never believe it could be so interesting. I felt so comfortable—I had never touched a keyboard in my life. It was wonderful.'

As a result, I did receive my bunch of flowers!

Notes and references

1 Robson, M. (ed.) (1985) *Quality Circles in Action*, Gower Publishing, London.

2 Kolb, D. (1984) *Experiential Learning*, Prentice-Hall, Hemel Hempstead.

Appendix Music
A

Baroque music recordings suitable for second concert readings are contained on the following sets:

LIND Relaxing with the Classics
  Volume one—Largo
  Volume two—Adagio
  Volume three—Pastorale
  Volume four—Andante
  Volume five—Pianisimo
  Music for imaging
  Romantic interlude

Optimalearning Classics
  Music for the Imagination and Creativity, No. 1
  Music for the Imagination and Creativity, No. 2
  Baroque Music No. 1
  Baroque Music No. 2

The above are available from Forge House, see Appendix D for addresses.

Recordings suitable for centring and relaxation are available from New World Cassettes (see Appendix D for details). They will send a full catalogue on request.

Some suggested titles are:

  The Enchanted Lake by Liadov
  Eventide by Steve Halpern
  Dawn by Steve Halpern
  Inner Light by Kessner and Helm
  Breathe by Bernoff and Allen
  Dreams of Atlantis by Naegele Music for an Inner Journey by Steve Bergman

The following are some of the titles, listed under activities, contained in the Viola set of music for trainers published by PLS in Bremen. A full list is to be found in the book *Viola* by Hartmut Wagner. The book, with a complete set of cassettes or CDs, is available from the SKILL Institute or from Forge House.

1 **Centring** (i.e. entering a state of relaxed awareness)
    James Galway: Into the Forest Kitaro
    Mannelli/Goldman: Silk Road
    Sky: Dreams
2 **Concert reading**
    Pachelbel: Canon in D
    Vivaldi: Concerto in C major PV 79 (Largo)
    Bach: Suite No. 3 in D major
    Handel: Firework music (La Paix)
3 **Energy raising**
    Vivaldi: Concerto C major PV 78 (Allegri)
    Mozart: Divertimento KV 136 (Allegro)
4 **Activation/breaks**
    Cusco: Virgin Islands
    Norbert Saric's B.O.B.S.: First Touch
    Smokie: *Needles and Pins*

Appendix B How clear is your mind's eye?

To find out what sort of an imager you are, complete the following questionnaire. Before you start, close your eyes, take a few deep breaths and carry out one of the relaxation exercises described in Chapter 9 (p. 79). Then open your eyes and read the first question.

Take your time. This is not a timed exercise. When the image has become as clear as you can make it, open your eyes and write down a rating, in accordance with the following scale:

Fairly clear   2
Vague but recognizable   1
Little or no image   0

1 Visual
Visualize the following:

1.1	A candle flame	☐
1.2	A red sunset	☐
1.3	Swans flying	☐
1.4	A hand writing a memo on a blackboard	☐
1.5	A red triangle on green paper	☐
1.6	A three-digit number, written in blue on a whiteboard	☐
1.7	An endless desert	☐
1.8	Waves breaking on a beach	☐
1.9	Yourself getting into a car	☐
1.10	The outside of the building you live in	☐

Score ___

2 Auditory
Imagine the following sounds:

2.1	A deep gong reverberating	☐
2.2	A telephone ringing	☐
2.3	A voice calling your name	☐
2.4	The noise of traffic	☐
2.5	Children playing	☐
2.6	A pigeon cooing	☐
2.7	A jet aeroplane passing overhead	☐

2.8   A stone falling into a lake   ☐
2.9   Voices in the next room   ☐
2.10   A favourite piece of music   ☐

                                                          Score ___

3 Kinesthetic
Imagine what it feels like to be:

3.1   Chopping wood energetically   ☐
3.2   Running slowly along a wet beach   ☐
3.3   Swimming in the sea   ☐
3.4   Playing a ball game   ☐
3.5   Driving a car   ☐

                                                          Score ___

4 Tactile
Imagine the feeling of touching:

4.1   Sandpaper   ☐
4.2   Silk   ☐
4.3   An orange   ☐
4.4   A cat   ☐
4.5   Someone's hand   ☐

                                                          Score ___

Total of kinesthetic and tactile   _____

Total score

Now add up the scores. If you have scored 50 or more, you already have the ability to create multi-sensory images and will be able to use them straight away. If you scored between 26–49, you have a reasonably good imaging ability and will be able to make use of it in many areas. You will, however, need to develop it. If you scored 25 or less, you will be unlikely to find imaging useful at the moment. You will need to develop the technique with regular practise over the period of weeks.

Appendix C   Awareness chart

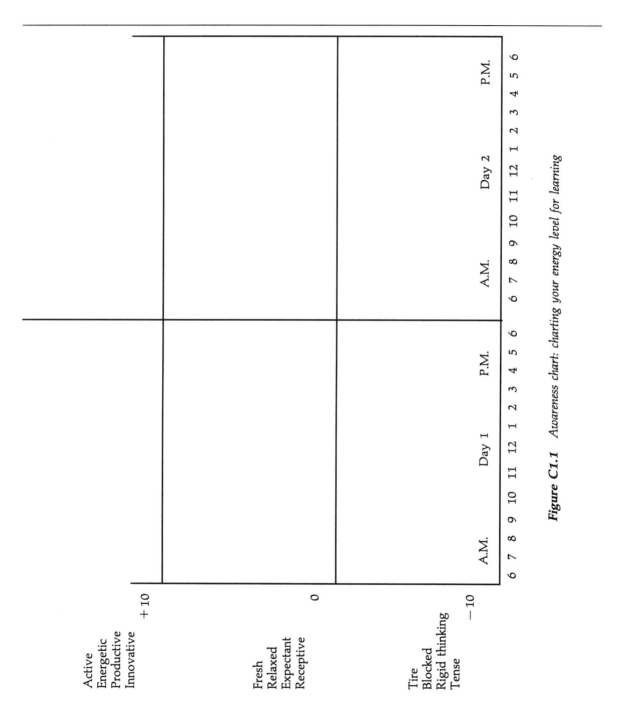

Figure C1.1 Awareness chart: charting your energy level for learning

Appendix D
Useful addresses

Accelerated Learning Systems Ltd., Univite House, 50 Aylesbury Road, Aston Clinton, Aylesbury, Bucks HP22 5AH (Tel: 01295 631177). Publishers of Accelerated Learning language courses and the *System 2000* Training and Development package.

The Actors' Institute, United Village, Carpenter's Mews, North Road, London N7 9EF (Tel: 0171 609 9221). They run a monthly weekend 'Mastery' course, which imparts basic acting skills.

The Alexander Technique: The Society of Teachers of the Alexander Technique, 10 London House, 266 Fulham Road, London SW10 9EL (Tel: 0171 351 0828). They provide a list of qualified local Alexander Technique teachers.

Anglo–American Book Company Ltd., Underwood, St. Clears, Carmarthen, Dyfed SA33 4NE (Tel: 01994 23040). For mail order supply of books related to NLP, Accelerated Learning and related subjects.

Brain Clubs Ltd. (also, The Buzan Organization Ltd., the 'Use your Head Club' and 'The Brain Foundation'), PO Box 1821, The Harleyford Manor Estate, Marlow, Bucks SL7 2YW (Tel: 01628 477004). Publishers of the *Use your Head* magazine and other material by Tony Buzan.

Brain Gym. For courses and books contact: Hendon Natural Health Centre, 12 Golders Rise, London NW4 2HR (Tel: 0181 202 9747).

The Herrmann Institute (UK), Towngate House, 219 Huddersfield Road, Shelley, Huddersfield, Yorks. HD8 8LB (Tel: 01484 607369/Fax: 01484 608428).

Inner Track Learning. For information about books, cassettes and courses contact: Centre for Language and Life Skills, Forge House, Kemble, Glos. GL7 6AD (Tel: 01285 770635).

Kingwood Centre for Learning, Badgemore, Henley on Thames, Oxon RG9 4NR (Tel: 01491 412488/Fax: 01491 412489).

London School of Puppetry, 2 Legard Road, London N5 1DE (Tel: 0171 359 7357). They run courses on the use of glove and other puppets.

Neuro-Linguistic Programming NLP. For information on membership, books, videos and courses contact: Sue Gazey, The Association for Neuro-Linguistic Programming, 48 Corser Street, Stourbridge, West Midlands DY8 2DQ (Tel: 01384 443935). For information on conferences contact: Jo Hogg, 27 Maury Road, London N16 7BP (Tel: 0181 806 6165).

New World Cassettes, Paradise Farm, Westhall, Halesworth, Suffolk IF19 8RH (Tel: 01986 781682). For the supply of music cassettes for relaxation and guided visualization.

SEAL (The Society for Effective Affective Learning), c/o Forge House, Kemble, Glos. GL7 6AD. For details of membership, conferences, workshops, books, cassettes and videos on Accelerated Learning and related methods.

Yoga. For teacher training courses on the use of Yoga in the classroom contact: RYE (Research on Yoga in Education), 70 Thurleigh Road, London SW12 (Tel: 0181 673 4869). For names of qualified local Yoga teachers contact: The British Wheel of Yoga, 1 Hamilton Place, Boston Road, Sleaford, Lincs. NG34 7ES (Tel: 01529 306851).

Bibliography

Adams, J. (1987) *Conceptual Blockbusting—A Guide to Better Ideas*, Penguin Books, London.

Ansell, G. (1984) 'Make the Most of your Memory', National Extension College Trust Ltd., Cambridge.

Bandler, R. (1985) *Using Your Brain—For a Change—Neuro-Linguistic Programming*, Real People Press, Moab, Utah USA.

Bandler, R. and Grinder, J. (1981) *Trance-formations*, Real People Press, Moab, Utah USA.

Barlow, W. (1973) *The Alexander Principle*, Arrow Books, London.

Beaver, D. (1994) *Lazy Learning*, Element Books Ltd., Shaftesbury, Dorset.

Bond, T. (1988) *Games for Social and Life Skills*, Hutchinson, London.

Bono, E. de (1982) *de Bono's Thinking Course*, BBC Publications, London.

Bourner, T., Martin, V. and Race, P. (1993) *Workshops that Work*, McGraw-Hill, Maidenhead.

Buzan, T. (1974) *Use Your Head*, BBC Books, London.

Buzan, T. (1988) *Make the Most of your Mind*, Pan Books, London.

Buzan, T. (1993) *The Mind Map Book*, BBC Books, London.

Casey, F. (1985) *How to Study—A Practical Guide*, Macmillan Education Ltd., Basingstoke.

Dennison, P. and Dennison, G. (1994) *Brain Gym for Business—Instant Brain Boosters for On-the-Job Success*, Edu-Kinesthetics Inc., Ventura, California.

DePorter, B. (1993) *Quantum Learning*, Piatkus Books, London.

Diamond, H. and Diamond, M. (1985) *Fit for Life*, Bantam Press, London.

Downes, S. and Perry, P. (1983) *Improve Your Learning*, Longman Group Ltd. and Manpower Services Commission, Harlow, Essex.

Dryden, G. and Voss, J. (1993) *The Learning Revolution*, Profile Books, Auckland, New Zealand.

Dudley, G. (1986) *Double Your Learning Power*, Thorsons Publishing Group, Wellingborough.

Elliott, K. and Wright, D. (publication undated) *Studying the Professional Way—The OUPUT Study Method*, Northwick Publishers, Worcester.

Evans, R. and Russell, P. (1989) *The Creative Manager*, Unwin Paperbacks, London.

Evers, S. (1993) 'The Manager as a Professional', The Institute of Management, Corby.

Ferrucci, P. (1982) *What we may be—The visions and techniques of psychosynthesis*, Turnstone Press, Wellingborough, Northants.

Friedberger, J. (1991) *Office Yoga*, Thorsons Publishing Group, Wellingborough.

Fritz, R. (1989) *The Path of Least Resistance—Learning to become the Creative Force in your own Life*, Fawcett Columbine, New York USA.

Gallwey, T. (1974) *The Inner Game of Tennis*, Bantam Books, London.

Gardner, H. (1983) *Frames of Mind—The Theory of Multiple Intelligences*, Paladin, London.

Gelb, M. (1981) *Body learning—An introduction to the Alexander Technique*, Aurum Press Ltd., London.

Gilling, D. and Brightwell, R. (1982) *The Human Brain*, Orbis Publications and the BBC, London.

Glouberman, D. (1989) *Life choices and life changes through imagework*, Unwin Hyman Ltd., London.

Good, M. and South, C. (1988) *In the know—8 keys to successful learning*, BBC Books, London.

Heron, J. (1989) *The Facilitator's Handbook*, Kogan Page, London.

Hodgkinson, L. and Piatkus, J. (1988) *The Alexander Technique and how it can help you*, Piatkus Books, London.

Hopson, B. and Scally, M. (1989) *Wake Up Your Brain—Creative Problem Solving*, Lifeskills, Leeds.

Jones, J. and Bearley, W. (1989) *Energizers for Training and Conferences*, Organization Design and Development Inc., King of Prussia, Pensylvania.

Kermani, K. (1990) *Autogenic Training*, Souvenir Press, London.

Lawlor, M. (1988) *Inner Track Learning*, Pilgrims Publications, Kemble.

Lazarus, A. (1984) *In the mind's eye—The power of imagery for personal enrichment*, The Guildford Press, New York USA.

Loye, D. (1983) *The Sphinx and the Rainbow*, New Science Library, London.

Lozanov, G. (1978) *Suggestology and Outlines of Suggestopedy*, Gordon and Breach Science Publishers, London.

Maltz, M. (1960) *Psycho-cybernetics*, Prentice Hall, Englewood Cliffs, New Jersey USA.

Marshall, L. and Rowland, F. (1981) *A Guide to Learning Independently*, The Open University Press, Milton Keynes.

Meredeen, S. (1988) *Study for Survival and Success—Guidenotes for College Students*, Paul Chapman Publishing Ltd., London.

Nierenberg, G. (1982) *The Art of Creative Thinking*, Simon & Schuster, New York USA.

Nolan, V. (1987) *The Innovator's Handbook*, Sphere Books Ltd., London.

O'Connor, J. and Seymour, J. (1993) *Introducing Neuro-Linguistic Programming*, Aquarian Press, Wellingborough.

O'Connor, J. and Seymour, J. (1994) *Training with NLP*, Thorsons Publishing Group, Wellingborough.

Odle, C. (1990) *Practical Visualization*, Aquarian Press, Wellingborough.

Oech, R. von (1983) *A whack on the side of the head*, Angus & Robertson, London.

Olson, R. (1978) *The Art of Creative Thinking*, Barnes & Noble Books, New York, USA.

Ostrander, S. and Schroeder, L. (1995) *Superlearning 2000*, Souvenir Press, London.

Page, M. (1990) *Visualization—the key to fulfilment*, Aquarian Press, Wellingborough.

Palmer, R. and Pope, C. (1984) *Brain Train—Studying for Success*, E. & F.N. Spon, London.

Robbins, A. (1986) *Unlimited Power*, Simon & Schuster, London.

Rogers, C. (1967) *On Becoming a Person*, Constable and Co., London.

Rogers, C. (1980) *A Way of Being*, Houghton Mifflin, Boston.

Rogers, C. (1983) *Freedom to Learn*, Macmillan, New York.

Rose, C., Gill, M-J. and Cassone, P. (1991) *Accelerated Learning System 2000: Training and Development Program*, Accelerated Learning Systems Ltd., Aylesbury.

Rose, C. and Goll, L. (1992) *Accelerate Your Learning*, Accelerated Learning Systems Ltd., Aylesbury.

Rowntree, D. (1983) *Learn how to study—A programmed guide for students of all ages*, Macdonald & Co. Ltd., London.

Russell, P. (1984) *The Brain Book*, Routledge & Kegan Paul, London.

Saraswati, S. S. (1982) 'Yoga Nidra', Bihar School of Yoga, Monghir, India. Available from Satyanandra Yoga Centre, London.

Senge, P. (1990) *The Fifth Discipline—The Art and Practice of the Learning Organization*, Century Business Books, London.

Senge, P., Roberts, C., Ross, R., Smith, B. and Kleiner, A. (1994) *The Fifth Discipline Fieldbook—Strategies and Tools for Building a Learning Organization*, Doubleday, New York USA.

Shone, R. (1984) *Creative Visualization*, Thorsons Publishing Group, Wellingborough.

Sommer, R. (1978) *The Mind's Eye—Imagery in Everyday Life*, Delta Publishing, New York USA.

Syer, J. and Connolly, C. (1991) *Think to Win*, Simon & Schuster, London.

Six editorial consultants (ed) (1982) *The Brain—A User's Manual*, New English Library, Sevenoaks, Kent.

Index

Page numbers in italic refer to mind maps and figures.

Accelerated Learning, 28, 87
Allied Dunbar, 156–160
Robson Rhodes, 160–166
Activities, 46–53, 162–165
  activity creation, 58
  advertisements
    design of, 59
  energy levels, control of, 82–83
    (*see also* Synergy)
  group, 46–47, 50–53, 163
    consultation in, 59
  individual, 47, 48–49, 58, 142–143
  materials creation, 59
  mental imagery, 58
  partnered, 47, 49–50, 58–59,
    162–163
    helping each other, 58
  plays, invention of, 60
  press releases, creation of, 60
  process oriented, 46
  review project, 59
  storytelling, 60
  task-oriented, 46
  teaching preparation, 58
  team-based, 50–53, 59–60
  television programmes, creation
    of, 60
Actor, performance by trainer, 89, 96
Adams, Henry, 121
Advertisements, design of, 59
Affective Programming, 123–125
Alexander, Mathias, 97
Alexander Technique, 7, 88–89,
  97–101
  directing, 98
  good use, 97–98
  inhibiting, 98

voice production, 99–101
Allied Dunbar:
  Accelerated Learning, use of,
    156–160
  case study, 155–160
Alpha state, in the brain, 89
Anchoring, in Neuro-Linguistic
  Programming, 116, 123
Atmosphere, of training sessions, 12,
  22, 30–32
Attitude, positive, 116
Audience:
  in training sessions, 12, 88
    body language of, 88, 106–107
    brain dominance of, 66, 71–72
    communication with, 87–88, 91
    emotional state of, 106
    energy levels of, 82–83, 106
    rapport with, 13, 22, 88, 106
    self-image, 115, 122–124
Audio tapes, use of, 40
Auditory mode of learning, 6, 37, 69,
  72, 82
Authentic behaviour, in group
  dynamics, 47
Authority, of trainer, 88
Autogenic Training, 7, 80
Autonomous mode, in training, 20,
  23, 57–61, 62

Baroque music, 29, 39, 79, 89–90,
  132, 167
Barriers, to learning, 4–5, 87, 95–96,
  122–124
Body:
  Alexander Technique, 7, 88–89,
    97–101

Body:
   Alexander Technique, *cont'd.*
      directing, 98
      good use, 97
      inhibiting, 98
      voice production, 99–101
   body–mind link, 7, 12, 76–84, 85,
      124
   body language, 88
      of audience, 106–107
   movement of, 95–99, *102*
Brain:
   alpha state, 89
   body–mind link, 7, 12, 76–84, 85,
      124
   brain dominance:
      of audience, 66, 71–72,
         105–106
      of trainer, 66, 71, 105
   Brain Gym, 7, 82–83
   Brain Map, 66
   capacity of, 4
   cerebral cortex, 5, 66
   concentration, 81–82
   double-planeness, 87–88
   energy in the body, 82–83, 124
      diet, 83–84
   function, inner awareness of
      trainer, 105–106
   Herrmann Brain Dominance
      Instrument (HBDI), 66,
      67–70, 73
   left hemisphere, 5, 65–66
   limbic system, 5–6, 66
   lower left quadrant B, 68
   lower right quadrant C, 68
   mid-brain, 5
   oxygen, supply of, 78, 124
   potential, *66*
   relaxation of, 78–82, 89–90, 124
   right hemisphere, 5, 65–66
   subconscious mind, germination of
      ideas, 142
   suggestion to, 87–92
   synergy, 148
   upper left quadrant A, 67–68
   upper right quadrant D, 69
   (*see also* Mind maps)
Brainstorming as a game, 143
Breathing, 78–79,
   concentration on, 81
   exercises, 79

British Association of Autogenic
      Training, 80
Card index, as memory aid, 133
Cerebral cortex, 5, 66
Chain of Links, as memory aid, 132
Children:
   inner child, as an aid to learning,
      90–91
Clairvoyant, the game of, 50
Closure, in group dynamics, 47
Colour, use of, 28
Communication :
   in organizations:
      quality circles, 155
   of trainer with audience, 87–88,
      91
Computer skills, case study, 160–166
Concentration:
   and the brain, 81–82
   in learning, 81–82, 129
Concert reading, 39–40, 89–90, 163
Confrontation dimension in
      facilitation, 20, 23, 24
Consciousness (*see* Brain)
Cooperative mode, in training, 20,
      23, 47
Crosswords, 51
Cybernetics, feedback in, 150

Defensiveness, in group dynamics,
      46–47
Definition match, the game of, 52
Dennison, Paul, 7
Dialogue:
   in group dynamics, 149
   in learning, 149
Dialogues, in training, 37–39
Diamond, Harvey, *Fit for Life*, 83
Diet, effect on energy levels, 83–84
Dimensions of facilitation:
   confronting, 20, 23, 24
   feeling, 20, 22
   meaning, 20, 22
   structuring, 21, 22
   valuing, 21, 22
Direction, use in the Alexander
      Technique, 98
Double-planeness in the brain, 87–88
Dryden, G., *The Learning Revolution*, 70

Educational Kinesiology (*see* Brain
      Gym)

Emotional state:
  of audience in training session, 106
  control of in learning, 81
Energy levels:
  of audience in training session, 82–83, 106
  control of, (*see also* Synergy)
    effect of diet, 83–84
    effect on the brain, 82–83, 124
    influence on learning, *171*
Engineering theory, servo-mechanisms, 150
Environment, importance of in training sessions, 12, 22, 28–30, 89, 156–157, 162
Environmental policies, 55–58
  visualization of, 116
Ethics, 55–58
  visualization of, 116
Evaluation, of training courses, 16
Exercises:
  for breathing, 79
  sitting, 78

Facilitation, 10–15
  confronting dimension, 20, 23, 24
  feeling dimension, 20, 22
  meaning dimension, 20, 22
  planning dimension, 20, 21
  structuring dimension, 21, 22
  valuing dimension, 21, 22
Fantasy land, the game of, 60
Feedback in cybernetics, 150
Feeling dimension in facilitation, 20, 22
Fit for Life, Harvey Diamond, 83
Flash cards, as memory aid, 133
Forcing connections, the game of, 142
Forecasting, of problems, 116
Four quadrant teaching cycle, 20–24, 25, 27–33, 34, 36–43, 44
  practice, 23, 46–53, 54
  preparation, 21–22, 26–33, 34
  presentation, 22–23, 35–43, 44
  primary activation, 47
Frames of Mind, Howard Gardner, 7, 70–71
Fritz, Robert, 139
  Technologies for creating, 147, 150

Gallwey, Timothy, *The Inner Game of Tennis*, 116

Games, 50–51, 90–91
  brainstorming, 143
  clairvoyant, 50
  crossword, 51
  definition match, 52
  fantasy land, 60
  forcing connections, 142
  group brain, 51
  group sculpture, 53
  hot ball, 50
  map what you know, 51
  memory mime, 52
  name game, 50
  outlandish ideas, 143
  paint a picture of success, 52
  sequence shuffle, 52
  stand or fall, 52
  super salesperson, 59–60
  television game show, 52
  terminology bingo, 51
  twenty questions, 59
  windmill, 51
  (*see also* Activities)
Gardner, Howard, *Frames of mind*, 7, 70–71
Gibran, Kahlil, *The Prophet*, 65
Glospot, a fictional case study, *xxiii–xxix*, 3–4, 10–11, 19–20, 26–27, 35–36, 45–46, 55–57, 65–66, 76–77, 86–87, 94–95, 103–104, 109–110, 121–122, 127–128, 139, 140, 146–147
Goals, in learning, 114, 123, 139–144, *145*
Goddard, R. H., 155
Good use, as an Alexander Technique method, 97–98
Graphics, use of, 30
Gregorc Thinking Style Test, 66
Group activities, 46–47, 50–53, 163
  consultation in, 59
Group brain, the game of, 51
Group dynamics, 46–53, 91
  authentic behaviour, 47
  closure in, 47
  defensiveness in, 46–47
  dialogue, 149
  'storming' in, 47
  team learning, 148
  trust in, 47
Group sculpture, the game of, 53

Hammarskjold, Dag, 86
HBDI (*see* Herrmann Brain
    Dominance Instrument)
HCP (*see* Hemisphere Centre Profile)
Health, as a factor in learning, 83–84
Hendon Natural Health Centre, 83
Hemisphere Centre Profile (HCP), 66
Hemispheres of the brain:
    left, 5, 65–66
    right, 5, 65–66
Herrmann Brain Dominance
    Instrument (HBDI), 66,
    67–70, 73
Heron, John, *The Facilitator's
    Handbook*, 20–24, 47, 57
Hierarchical mode, in training, 20, 22
Hot ball, the game of, 50

Imagination, use of in learning (*see*
    Visualization)
Individual activities, 47, 48–49, 58,
    142–143
Infantilization (*see* Inner child)
Inhibiting, as an Alexander
    Technique method, 98
Inner awareness:
    of self by trainer, 13, 105–107,
      108, 143
      brain function, 105–106
      emotional state, 104–105, 106
      learning mode, 106
      physical state, 104–105
Inner child, as an aid to learning, 90–
    91
Inner Game of Tennis, The, Timothy
    Gallwey, 116
Institute of Management, *Code of
    Conduct*, 57
Intelligence, 65–74, 75, 130–132
    children, 90–91
    Herrmann Brain Dominance
      Instrument, 67–70, 73
    inter-personal, 7, 70, 73, 131
    intra-personal, 7, 70, 131
    kinesthetic, 7, 70, 81, 131
    linguistic, 7, 70, 130
    mathematical/logical, 7, 70, 130
    multiple, 70–73
    musical, 7, 70, 130
    study skills, 127–128
    systems thinking, 150
    visual/spatial, 7, 70, 81, 130 (*see*

also Visualization)
Inter-personal intelligence, 7, 70, 131
Intra-personal intelligence, 7, 70, 131
Introductions, to training sessions,
    30–32

Jacobson method of relaxation, 79–80
James, William, 94
Jung, Carl, 103

Kermani, Kai, *Autogenic Training*, 80
Kinesthetic learning, 6, 7, 37, 46–53,
    69, 72, 73, 81, 88, 131
Kolb, D., *Experiential Learning*, 166

Language, use of by trainer, 91, 95
Languages:
    Baroque music, as an aid to
      learning, 132
    learning of, 132–133
Learner-centred training, 13
Learning, 65–73, 75, 128–134
    Accelerated Learning, 28, 87,
      121–122
      Allied Dunbar, use of, 156–160
    Affective Programming, 123–125
    auditory, 6, 37, 69, 72, 82
    barriers to, 4–5, 87, 95–96,
      122–124
    body–mind link, 76–84, *85*, 124
    concentration, 81–82, 129
    dialogue, 149
    emotional control in, 81
    energy levels, importance of,
      82–83, 124, 171
    facilitation of, 10–15, 20–21
    goals in, 114, 123, 139–144, *145*
    health as a factor, 83–84
    Herrmann Brain Dominance
      Instrument, 67–70, 73
    inner child, role in, 90–91
    kinesthetic, 6, 37, 46–53, 69, 72,
      81, 88
    languages, 132–133
      Baroque music, use of, 132
    lifestyle as a factor, 83–84
    organizational cultures, 146–150,
      152
    posture, effect of, 78
    practice, 134
    relaxation in, 78–82, 89–90,
      111–112

Learning, *cont'd.*
　sleep, importance of, 83
　stress as an inhibitor of, 76–84
　suggestion in, 87–92, *93*
　　affirmation, 91–92
　　structural tension, 140–142
　team learning, 148–149
　visualization, 91–92, 109–117,
　　118, 132, 140–144
　visual, 6, *36–37, 41–43, 69, 72, 82,*
　　110, 164 (*see also*
　　Visualization)
Learning Revolution, The, G. Dryden,
　70
Letter-writing skills, case study,
　156–160
Lifestyle:
　creative orientation in, 147
　factor in learning, 83–84
　mental models, awareness of, 148
　personal mastery in, 147–148
　systems thinking, approach to, 150
Limbic system, 5–6, 66
Linguistic intelligence, 7, 70, 130
Loci System, 132
LOTUS 123, case study in training,
　160–166
Lozanov, Georgi, 7, 11, 28, 39, 87–92

Mammalian brain, 5
Map what you know, the game of,
　51
Mason, John, 45
Matching, *xvii*, 13, 15
Materials creation, as an activity, 59
Mathematical/logical intelligence, 7,
　70, 130
May, Rollo, 55
Meaning dimension in facilitation,
　20, 22
Meier, David, 3
Memory:
　card index, 133
　Chain of Links, 132
　flash cards, 133
　improvement of, 116, 132–133
　inner child, 90–91
　Loci System, 132
　mnemonic, 132, 163
　study skills, 127–128
　T for 1, 132
　testing of by self, 133–134

　visualization, 132
Memory mime, the game of, 52
Mental imagery, as an activity, 58
　(*see also* Visualization)
Mental models, of the world, 148
Metaphors, use of, 40
Mid-brain, 5
Mind (*see* Brain)
Mind maps, 36, 127–128, 129, 131,
　examples of, *9, 16, 25, 34, 37, 62,*
　75, 85, 93, 102, 108, 118, 126,
　136, 145
Mnemonic, 132, 163
Multiple intelligences, 7, 70–73
Music, use of, 28–30, 39, 79, 89–90,
　132, 164, 167–168
Musical intelligence, 7, 70, 130

Name game, 50
Neuro-Linguistic Programming, 6,
　13, 15, 88, 91
　anchoring, 116, 123
　well-formed outcome, 141
NLP(*see* Neuro-Linguistic
　Programming)

Office yoga, 7
Organizations:
　Allied Dunbar, case study, 155–160
　learning in, 146–150, 152
　quality circles, 155
　Robson Rhodes, case study,
　　160–166
　shared vision in, 148
　team learning, 148
Outlandish ideas, use of as a game,
　143
Oxygen, supply of to the brain, 78,
　124

Paint a picture of success, the game
　of, 52
Partnered activities, 47, 49–50,
　58–59, 162–163
　helping each other, 58
Performance, as a training technique,
　55–60, 62
　Allied Dunbar, case study,
　　159–160
　Robson Rhodes, case study,
　　165–166
Personal mastery, in life, 147–148

Piaget, Jean, 127
Pictures, use of, 30
Planning
    dimension in facilitation, 20, 21
    by trainer, 141–142, 143–144
Plays, invention of as an activity, 60
Positive attitude, development of, 116
Posture, effect on learning, 78, 88–89, 96–101
Practice:
    in the four quadrant teaching cycle, 20–24, 25, 36–43, 54
    of learning, 134
    as a training technique, 46–53, 54
        Allied Dunbar, case study, 158–159
        Robson Rhodes, case study, 165
Preparation:
    in the four quadrant teaching cycle, 21–22, 26–33, 34
    as a training technique, 27–33, 34
        Allied Dunbar, case study, 156–157
        Robson Rhodes, case study, 161–162
Presentation:
    in the four quadrant teaching cycle, 22–23, 35–43, 44
    as a training technique, 22–23, 36–43, 44
        Allied Dunbar, case study, 157–158
        Robson Rhodes, case study, 162–165
Press releases, creation of as an activity, 60
Primary activation, in the four quadrant teaching cycle, 47
Problem forecasting, 116
Process oriented activities, 46
Prophet, The, Gibran Kahlil, 65

Quadrant teaching cycle, four stage, 20–24, 25, 27–33, 34, 36–43, 44
    practice, 23, 46–53, 54
    preparation, 21–22, 26–33, 34
    presentation, 22–23, 35–43, 44
    primary activation, 47
Quadrants of the brain:
    lower left B, 68
    lower right C, 68
    upper left A, 67–68
    upper right D, 69
Quality circles, 155

Rapport, of trainer with audience, 13, 22, 88, 106
Relaxation and learning, 78–82, 89–90, 111–112
    Alexander Technique, 7, 88–89, 97–101
        directing, 98
        good use, 97
        inhibiting, 98
        voice production, 99–101
    Autogenic Training, 80, 89, 90
    breathing, 78–79
    emotional control, 81
    Jacobson method, 79–80
    posture, 78
    sitting exercises, 78
    Transcendental Meditation (TM), 82
    yoga, 80–81, 89, 90
Review project as an activity, 59
Revision, use of in study skills, 133–134
Robson Rhodes:
    Accelerated Learning, use of, 160–166
    case study, 160–166
Rogers, Carl, 10, 26
Role-play, as a training technique, 37–39

Self-image, of audience in training session, 115, 122–124
Self-testing, of memory, 133–134
Senge, Peter, *The fifth discipline*, 147, 150
Shweitzer, Albert, 109
Sensory acuity, in training, 88
Sensory modalities, 6, 70, 72, 106
    questionnaire, test of ability
Sequence shuffle, the game of, 52
Servo-mechanisms, in engineering theory, 150
Sitting exercises, as an aid to relaxation, 78
Skills training, 116
Sleep, importance of in learning, 83
Smoking, in the training context, 84
Sperry, Roger, 19

Stand or fall, the game of, 52
Stories, use of, 40
'Storming', in group dynamics, 47
Storytelling as an activity, 60
Stress:
  in learning:
    causes of, 77–78
    management of, 76, 84
    symptoms of, 77
Structuring dimension in facilitation,
    21, 22
Students (*see* Training: audience)
Study skills, 121–124, *125*, 127–135,
    136, 145
  intelligence, 127–128
  memory, 127–128
  mind maps, use of, 127–128, 129
  revision, 133–134
  targets, 139–144
  (*see also* Learning)
Subconscious mind, germination of
    ideas, 142
Suggestion as a training technique,
    87–92, *93*, 122–125
  affirmation, 91–92, 123
  structural tension, 140–142
  visualization, 91–92, 109–117,
    118, 123–124, 129, 132,
    140–144, 164
Suggestopedia, 39, 87–92
Super salesperson, the game of, 59–60
Synergy, 148
Systems thinking intelligence, 150

Tension (*see* Relaxation)
T for 1, as memory aid, 132
Targets, use of in study skills,
    139–144
Task-oriented activities, 46
Teaching cycle, four quadrant, 20–24,
    25, 27–33, *34*, 36–43, *44*
  practice, 23, 46–53, 4
  preparation, 21–22, 26–33, *34*
  presentation, 22–23,35–43, *44*
  primary activation, 47
Teaching preparation as an activity, 58
Team-based activities, 50–53, 59–60
Team learning, in group dynamics,
    148–149
Technologies for Creating, Robert Fritz,
    147,150
Technology, use of, 14, 40

Television game show, 52
Television programmes, creation of
    as an activity, 60
Tennyson, Lord Alfred , 146
Terminology bingo, the game of, 51
TM (*see* Transcendental Meditation)
Transcendental Meditation (TM), 82
Trainer:
  as actor, 89, 96
  authority of, 88
  body movement of, 95, 96–99,105
  brain dominance of, 66, 72, 105
  inner awareness of, 13, 105–107,
    108, 143
    brain function, 105–106
    emotional state, 104–105, 106
    learning mode, 106
    physical state, 104–105
  language, use of, 91, 95
  planning, importance of, 141–142,
    143–144
  visualization, use of by self,
    141–144
  voice, control of, 95, 99–101
Training:
  activities, use of, 46–53
  Allied Dunbar, case study of,
    156–160
  atmosphere, importance of, 12, 22,
    30–32
  audience, 12, 88
    body language of, 88, 106–107
    brain dominance of, 66, 71–72,
    105–106
    communication with, 87–88, 91
    emotional state of, 106
    energy levels of, 82–83, 106
    rapport with, 13, 22, 88, 106
    self-image, 115, 122–124
  Autogenic Training, 7, 80
  autonomous mode, 20, 23, 57–61,
    62
  computer skills, case study of,
    160–166
  cooperative mode, 20, 23, 47
  confronting dimension of
    facilitation, 20, 23, 24
  dialogues, use of, 37–39
  environment, importance of, 12,
    22, 28–30, 89, 156–157, 162
  feeling dimension of facilitation,
    20, 22

Trainer, *cont'd.*
  four-quadrant teaching cycle,
    20–24, 25, 27–33, *34*
  hierarchical mode, 20, 22
  introductions to, 30–32
  learner-centred, 13
  letter-writing skills, case study of,
    156–160
  LOTUS 123, case study of,
    160–166
  meaning dimension of facilitation,
    20, 22
  performance, 55–60, *62*
    Allied Dunbar, case study,
      159–160
    Robson Rhodes, case study,
      165–166
  planning dimension of facilitation,
    20, 21
  practice, 46–53, *54*
    Allied Dunbar, case study,
      158–159
    Robson Rhodes, case study, 165
  preparation, 27–33, *34*
    Allied Dunbar, case study,
      156–157
    Robson Rhodes, case study,
      161–162
  presentation, 22–23, 36–43, *44*
    Allied Dunbar, case study,
      157–158
    Robson Rhodes, case study,
      162–165
    Robson Rhodes, case study,
      160–166
  role play, use of, 37–39
  sensory acuity, 88
  skills training, 116
  smoking, 84
  stress, awareness of, 76–84
  structuring dimension of
    facilitation, 21, 22

students (*see* Training: audience)
suggestion, 87–92, *93*, 122–125
  affirmation, 91–92, 123
  visualization, 91–92, 123–124,
    129, 164
Suggestopedia, 39, 87–92
technology, use of, 14, 40
valuing dimension of facilitation,
  21, 22
(*see also* Learning, facilitation)
Training courses:
  evaluation, 16
  joining instructions, 27, 156, 161
Trust, in group dynamics, 47
Twenty questions, the game of, 59

Valuing dimension in facilitation, 21,
  22
Video tapes, use of, 40
Voice :
  control by trainer, 95, 99–101
  production, *102*
    use of Alexander Technique,
    99–101
Visual learning, 6, 36–37, 41–43, 69,
  72, 82, 110, 164
Visual-spatial intelligence, 7, 70,
  81
Visualization, 6, 12, 41–43, 70–72,
  78, 91–92, 106, 109–117,
  123–125, 129, 132, 140–142,
  147–148
  as memory aid, 132
  structural tension, 140–144, 148,
    150

Well-formed outcome, in Neuro-
  Linguistic Programming,
  141
Windmill, the game of, 51

Yoga, 80–81

Further titles in the McGraw-Hill Training Series

WORKSHOPS THAT WORK
100 Ideas to Make Your Training Events More Effective
Tom Bourner, Vivien Martin, Phil Race
ISBN 0-07-707800-4

THE HANDBOOK FOR ORGANIZATIONAL CHANGE
Strategy and Skill for Trainers and Developers
Carol A. O'Connor
ISBN 0-07-707693-1

TRAINING FOR PROFIT
A Guide to the Integration of Training in an Organization's
Success
Philip Darling
ISBN 0-07-707786-5

TEAM BUILDING
A Practical Guide for Trainers
Neil Clark
ISBN 0-07-707846-2

DEVELOPING MANAGERS AS COACHES
A Trainer's Guide
Frank Salisbury
ISBN 0-07-707892-6

THE ASSERTIVE TRAINER
A Practical Guide for Trainers
Liz Willis and Jenny Daisley
ISBN 0-07-709077-2

MEETING MANAGEMENT
A Manual of Effective Training Material
Leslie Rae
ISBN 0-07-707782-2

LEARNING THROUGH SIMULATIONS
A Guide to the Design and Use of Simulations in Business and
Education
John Fripp
ISBN 0-07-707588-9 paperback
ISBN 0-07-707789-X Disk

IMAGINATIVE EVENTS Volumes I & II
A Sourcebook of Innovative Simulations, Exercises, Puzzles
and Games
Ken Jones
ISBN 0-07-707679-6 Volume I
ISBN 0-07-707680-X Volume II
ISBN 0-07-707681-8 Set Ringbinder

TRAINING TO MEET THE TECHNOLOGY CHALLENGE
Trevor Bentley
ISBN 0-07-707589-7

CLIENT-CENTRED CONSULTING
A Practical Guide for Internal Advisers and Trainers
Peter Cockman, Bill Evans and Peter Reynolds
ISBN 0-07-707685-0

TOTAL QUALITY TRAINING
The Quality Culture and Quality Trainer
Brian Thomas
ISBN 0-07-707472-6

CAREER DEVELOPMENT AND PLANNING
A Guide for Managers, Trainers and Personnel Staff
Malcolm Peel
ISBN 0-07-707554-4

DESIGNING AND ACHIEVING COMPETENCY
A Competency-based Approach to Developing People and
Organizations
Edited by Rosemary Boam and Paul Sparrow
ISBN 0-07-707572-2

SELF-DEVELOPMENT
A Facilitator's Guide
Mike Pedler and David Megginson
ISBN 0-07-707460-2

DEVELOPING WOMEN THROUGH TRAINING
A Practical Handbook
Liz Willis and Jenny Daisley
ISBN 0-07-707566-8

HOW TO SUCCEED IN EMPLOYEE DEVELOPMENT
Moving from Vision to Results
Ed Moorby
ISBN 0-07-707459-9

MAKING MANAGEMENT DEVELOPMENT WORK
Achieving Success in the Nineties
Charles Margerison
ISBN 0-07-707382-7

MANAGING PERSONAL LEARNING AND CHANGE
A Trainer's Guide
Neil Clark
ISBN 0-07-707344-4

THE BUSINESS OF TRAINING
Achieving Success in Changing World Markets
Trevor Bentley
ISBN 0-07-707328-2

All books are published by:

McGraw-Hill Book Company Europe
Shoppenhangers Road, Maidenhead, Berkshire SL6 2QL, England
Tel: (01628) 23432   Fax: (01628) 770224